'This is a brave book. It takes a subject hardly ever discussed in global business, gay rights, and blows apart misconceptions.'

Martha Lane Fox, Founder lastminute.com

'Lord Browne has written a book of unflinching honesty and lasting social value. In it he says, 'You will do more to better the world when you can be authentic.' It took much of his remarkable career for him to reach that conclusion; but in doing so, he makes it infinitely easier for others to follow.'

Sir Martin Sorrell, CEO WPP

'Despite much progress in recent years, gay rights issues around the world remain a serious problem. *The Glass Closet* by John Browne is a brave and fascinating book that shows how businesses can lead the way in promoting gay rights and why being yourself is best for business and for you.'

Sir Richard Branson, Chairman Virgin Group

'How many of your people are living a double life? How many are wasting energy and emotion keeping their closet closed? Business leaders are used to shaping their worlds, to making a difference. This is one place we can, and should.'

Peter Sands, CEO Standard Chartered

'Personal and instructive, *The Glass Closet* provides a compelling roadmap to what, as a society and as individuals, we can achieve if LGBT men and women are completely free from prejudice and anxiety because of who they are.'

Lloyd Blankfein, Chairman and CEO Goldman Sachs

'A courageous and salutary reminder that despite huge progress we still have a long way to go to create the kind of tolerant and inclusive society of which business – as this book powerfully argues – must be a driving force.'

Paul Polman, CEO Unilever

'I commend John for sharing so openly his experience and insights – which are all too familiar to me – to stimulate a broader dialogue that is needed.'

Beth Brooke, Global Vice Chair Public Policy EY

'*The Glass Closet* is a wonderfully reflective, refreshingly candid account of the remarkable life and times of Lord John Browne who, until he "came out", lived an increasingly uncomfortable double life – rising to the chief executive's suite as a highly successful corporate leader, while staying in the closet as a gay man until late in his professional life.'

General David H. Petraeus, US Army (retired)

'John Browne courageously illustrates how prejudice confines us and fails us ethically and economically. I am full of admiration for the way he has turned his story of disgrace and loss into a parable for our times.'

Sir Anish Kapoor, sculptor

THE GLASS CLOSET

Why Coming Out is Good Business

JOHN BROWNE

2 4 6 8 10 9 7 5 3

Published in 2014 by WH Allen, an imprint of Ebury Publishing
A Random House Group Company

The Random House Group Limited Reg. No. 954009

Addresses for companies within the Random House Group can be found at www.randomhouse.co.uk

A CIP catalogue record for this book is available from the British Library

The Random House Group Limited supports the Forest Stewardship Council® (FSC®), the leading international forest-certification organisation. Our books carrying the FSC label are printed on FSC®-certified paper. FSC is the only forest-certification scheme supported by the leading environmental organisations, including Greenpeace. Our paper procurement policy can be found at www.randomhouse.co.uk/environment

Typeset by e-type, Liverpool
Printed and bound in Great Britain by Clays Ltd, St Ives PLC

HB ISBN 9780753555316
TPB ISBN 9780753555323

To buy books by your favourite authors and register for offers visit
www.randomhouse.co.uk

To K da Mula

CONTENTS

DISCOVER MORE AT GLASSCLOSET.ORG

PROLOGUE

IN NOVEMBER 2012, during a break between votes in the House of Lords, I stood in a corridor talking to an academic, a bishop and a politician. I mentioned that the following morning I would moderate a panel at 'Out on the Street', an event at which senior business leaders would discuss ways of improving the climate for lesbian, gay, bisexual and transgender employees in the financial services sector. The trio of luminaries looked perplexed. 'How unusual,' one of them said. 'This problem is already solved. We don't have any problems at all in academic life, the Church and politics.'

It sounds like the start of a bad joke, but their collective astonishment is no laughing matter. There is a lack of awareness, even among highly educated people, of the difficulties that still plague LGBT employees. Despite the context set by significantly improved measures to reduce discrimination, changing attitudes towards gay marriage and the increasing visibility of gay figures in popular culture, it is estimated that 41 per cent of LGBT employees in the US remain closeted at work.[1] In the UK, the figure is 34 per cent.[2] Those aiming for the top certainly lack role models: at the end of 2013, there was not a single openly gay chief executive in the Fortune 500.

This book strives to understand what holds them back, and to convey the benefits that come with authenticity.

It is the culmination of more than a year of research and interviews with over 100 business professionals, executives, academics, sports and entertainment personalities, psychologists and diversity thought leaders from around the world. It has two goals. The first is to demonstrate, through my own story and the stories of other gay executives, that coming out is best for employees and the companies that support them. The second is to suggest a path that businesses can follow to foster values of authenticity, inclusion, diversity and respect.

There are some important caveats. First, I do not intend to speak for the entire gay community. The experience of coming out varies from person to person. It is shaped by factors including age, region, occupation, level of seniority, religious background and family circumstances. In soliciting interviews, I drew from my personal network, but I also cast the net wider to capture a greater range of voices and experiences. Even so, the book focuses primarily on white-collar professionals. This is not meant to obscure the challenges faced by blue-collar workers. The reality is that I have spent more than four decades in business. I wanted to write about that with which I am most familiar.

For similar reasons, this book focuses primarily on the US and Europe. The struggles faced by LGBT business people in the West pale into insignificance compared to those faced by gay men and women in countries where homosexuality is still criminalised, and where being exposed can lead to imprisonment or even death. While activists in the US argue the case for benefits for same-sex partners and legal recognition of same-sex marriage, activists in places such as Uganda and India are fighting for the most basic protections and rights. Their struggles deserve global attention, but are beyond the central scope of this book. It is my hope that business leaders and corporations in the West can use their influence to effect change for LGBT people elsewhere.

Finally, this book is meant to be practical rather than theoretical. The stories contained in these pages offer examples from which men and women can learn and selectively apply to their lives.

The act of coming out happens in a moment, but gaining the confidence to do so can take decades. The factors underlying that process cut across history and psychology, law and religion, triumph and failure. This book seeks to do the same. Chapter 1 centres on my resignation from BP, which resulted from revelations connected to my sexual orientation. The dramatic events that surrounded my departure marked a turning point in both my professional and personal life. They demonstrate the consequences of not being authentic.

My insecurity about my sexuality was not rooted solely in my upbringing, my business or my social networks. It was also heavily influenced by the long history of society perceiving and treating gay people differently. Chapter 2 introduces the historical context that has allowed homophobia to take root in societies across borders and time.

Homophobia, and the anti-gay laws it nurtured, is diminishing. Yet its legacy still colours our thinking today. In Chapter 3, we hear from closeted men and women who remain fearful that coming out will limit their chances of professional success. Their fears may seem overblown, but it is difficult to be balanced when you are living in the closet. Listening to their stories, I recognise much of my own experience.

Their concerns are steeped in an unfortunate truth: prejudice against gay people still exists. As we will see in Chapter 4, prejudice has diminished over time, but LGBT employees must always accept a degree of risk when coming out. Business, like any other pursuit, has its share of bigots. But it is also filled with a growing number of supporters. Chapter 5 illustrates why and how corporations are embracing change. They now understand the benefits of not just tolerating LGBT employees but actively courting them.

Since coming out I have lived much more freely and embraced new professional challenges without the anxiety of the closet. But coming out was a tough process. In Chapter 6, gay business people share their stories of the benefits of coming out. These stories are as varied as the people who make up the LGBT community.

The challenges of being authentic differ from sector to sector. With that in mind, in Chapter 7, I turn to fields beyond traditional business. These include professional sport, which lags behind the rest of society on LGBT equality and inclusion, and politics, one of the most important platforms from which to drive change. These are particular fields with exceptional circumstances, but they offer lessons applicable to gay men and women in other sectors.

This journey, from the closet to the chief executive's suite, will show us what companies can do to foster LGBT inclusion, which is the focus of Chapter 8. It will also demonstrate why gay employees must take responsibility for their own careers. If a company opens the closet door, it is up to the employee to walk through it.

I wish I had been brave enough to come out earlier during my tenure as chief executive of BP. I regret it to this day. I know that if I had done so, I would have made more of an impact for other gay men and women. It is my hope that the stories in this book will give some of them the courage to make an impact of their own.

CHAPTER ONE

HIDE-AND-SEEK

IT WAS TIME to leave the building.

At 5pm on 1 May 2007, just a few hours after resigning as chief executive of BP, I stepped into the elevator on the fifth floor of the London headquarters and began my descent. When the doors opened I had two options. I could make my way to an underground parking garage without being noticed and escape by car through a side exit on Charles II Street. Alternatively, I could simply walk through the lobby and out of the main entrance overlooking leafy St James's Square, where about thirty press photographers had spent the day waiting like vultures for their prey.

My overwhelming desire to conceal my sexual orientation over four decades in the oil industry had culminated in this terrible juncture. My long-kept secret was about to be exposed and I was not going to hide any longer. I decided that I would leave through the front door.

The photographers and editors back at their offices had plenty to feed on. At around ten o'clock that morning, reporting restrictions on a High Court injunction granted by Mr Justice Eady in January that year had been lifted. That decision would allow Associated Newspapers, publishers of the *Daily Mail*, *The Mail on Sunday* and *Evening Standard*, to disclose details of a three-year relationship I had with a young Canadian named Jeff Chevalier.

Rumours concerning our relationship had swirled about for months,[1] but the very public confirmation of that gossip would take most in the business world by surprise.

In 2003, Jeff was a twenty-three-year-old male escort. I met him on a now-defunct website. As a businessman in the public eye, I was too frightened to go out to a club or to find a date because of the risk of being discovered. Instead, I chose a secretive and far riskier approach. In any event, after nine months, he moved in with me. Too ashamed to tell most of my closest friends how we had met, we concocted a story that we had bumped into each other while running in Battersea Park, which was opposite my apartment on the other side of the River Thames. I never volunteered this to people, but naturally friends are curious. When pressed, I had my cover story.

The relationship eventually fell apart. I continued to support Jeff financially, not because I wanted to buy his silence but because, out of a sense of decency, I did not want to cut him off too summarily. I was not, however, willing to finance his life indefinitely. After about another nine months, I stopped sending him money. He started to send me text messages and emails. I ignored them. An email he sent on Christmas Eve of 2006 seemed like a threat. 'The least I am asking for is some assistance,' it said. 'I do not want to embarrass you, but I am being cornered by your lack of response to my myriad attempts at communication.'[2] I ignored this as well.

Christmas and New Year came and went. On Friday 5 January 2007, I was on holiday in Barbados when the *The Mail on Sunday* telephoned the BP press office. They said they intended to publish an exposé about my private life, focusing on how I met Jeff and detailing the time we spent together. Jeff had sold them the story for a substantial sum of money. They wanted me to comment by the end of the day.

Regardless of whether I did, they were going to publish their story on Sunday.

Thoughts of sand and sunshine gave way to anger and fear. The young man I had once trusted had chosen to sell our stories for money. Many of these stories would turn out to be exaggerated or wrong. The walls I had built around my private life started to crumble. I feared a chain reaction would start that would damage my life, my business relationships, my reputation and ultimately BP, the corporation that I had been trusted to lead. After emergency discussions with friends and colleagues, I decided to hire a top London law firm and seek an injunction to block publication of the story.

I was fifty-nine years old, and I had not discussed my sexual orientation with most of those closest to me. Yet I suddenly found myself explaining my situation to an unknown lawyer on my mobile phone. We had never met, but in a state of anxiety and stress I was being asked to share with him the most intimate details of my second, secret life. Perhaps that is why I decided not to tell the whole truth. When he asked how I had first come into contact with Jeff, I said we had met running in Battersea Park.

On Saturday 6 January, the High Court issued the injunction blocking the publication of the story. I felt a great relief, but knew it was fleeting. I knew that the newspaper would appeal the decision and doggedly work to have the injunction lifted. I also knew that my witness statement contained a single but important fabrication.

The next day I flew on to Trinidad for business. During my meetings with Prime Minister Patrick Manning, I was preoccupied with the injunction and the imminent publication of a damning report on safety at BP's refineries. I made up my mind that I could not continue as chief executive. The brewing storm around my personal life had the potential to destroy my reputation and I refused to let it have an impact on BP. On 8 January, I flew back to London on an overnight flight. After landing, I went to see the chairman of the board, Peter Sutherland. I explained to him as much as I could without divulging the substance or details of the injunction, as instructed by my lawyers. I said that I wanted to resign immediately. Although Peter accepted my proposal, the board decided that I would stay on until the end of July. With the injunction still working its way through the court system, and with all parties legally bound to silence, how could my resignation be explained to the public? The company named Tony Hayward as my successor. He would take over in the summer and I would have to wait.

On 16 January 2007, BP released the findings of the *Baker Report*, an investigation by a panel headed by former US Secretary of State James Baker into the March 2005 explosion at its Texas City refinery. My personal worries paled into insignificance. Fifteen people had died and more than 170 had been injured in that tragedy, one of the worst workplace accidents in the US in two decades. It was a very tense day on which I again accepted responsibility. The press conference stirred memories of my visit to the refinery in the immediate aftermath of the explosion, and of the anguish felt by the victims' families and our employees.

I was well practised at keeping my personal life separate from my professional life, but the brutal honesty of the report transcended the divide. The reality dawned on me that my fabrication of how I met Jeff was a lie. I was unable to concentrate on anything else. By 20 January 2007, I had corrected my witness statement and apologised to the High Court for misleading it. I was relieved to have done so, even though I knew in my heart that it would make no difference to the outcome.

To the outside world, business carried on as usual. My calendar for the following six months read like any other period of my life as chief executive of BP. Every day was filled with meetings and trips for business: five to New York, three to other US cities, two to Russia (including one to say farewell to Vladimir Putin) and one to China. There were also three BP board meetings and one annual general meeting during that time. I remained cool on the surface, but those were the most stressful days I have ever lived through.

At times, the weight of remaining silent made me act out of character. I cancelled my attendance at the World Economic Forum in Davos without giving a reason. In late January, I took a week off and simply disappeared, something I had never done before. In a state of heightened paranoia, I wanted to get away from anyone who might ask why I was leaving BP, and I escaped to stay with friends near Barcelona. I came back to hear that the High Court had ruled that the injunction should be lifted, but allowed it to stay in place temporarily pending an appeal. The Court of Appeal heard my appeal *in camera* on 5 and 6 March. While waiting for their judgement, I went to do some business in New York. I remember being so frozen with anxiety that I failed to appear in front of a CNBC camera crew waiting to film me for a business award. Jeff Immelt, the CEO of GE, the owner of CNBC, later called to say they had withdrawn the award.

Days later I lost my appeal, but again the court temporarily kept the injunction in place whilst I sought permission to appeal to the House of Lords in a final effort to protect my privacy. However, I knew this was unlikely to succeed and that the injunction would ultimately be lifted. Preparation for that event did not take up much time. It was as if all of it, including my resignation, was part of a schedule planned well in advance.

Those were the most nightmarish few months of my life. I was not a victim. We must own up to our choices and I had made some bad ones. I had lived in the closet and got myself into a mess with an escort. That was bad enough. But worse, I maintained the relationship and was not prepared to tell anyone about it. That led me to make a false witness statement, which I corrected after two weeks. It was not perjury, but it was close. The lie made things worse. Throughout the ordeal, my lawyers advised me that I must not discuss the case with anyone, but time enabled editors at *The Mail on Sunday* to elaborate their story. And time tortured me until the morning of 1 May 2007, when the injunction was finally lifted.

By noon, I had announced my resignation from BP, the company I had led for twelve years and the place where I had begun my career while still an undergraduate. My statement to the press had a tone of mourning.

'For the past forty-one years of my career at BP, I have kept my private life separate from my business life,' it said. 'I have always regarded my sexuality as a personal matter, to be kept private. It is a matter of personal disappointment that a newspaper group has now decided that allegations about my personal life should be made public.'

The announcement triggered tsunamis of headlines and stories that would dominate the front pages of UK and major international newspapers for days. By releasing the injunction, the High Court gave the press the freedom to publish a tangled skein of allegations, some of which were erroneous and misleading. I had not divulged details of sensitive discussions with Prime Minister Tony Blair and Chancellor of the Exchequer Gordon Brown to my ex-boyfriend as claimed. Nor had I misused company assets and funds to support him, a fact BP confirmed after reviewing the evidence.

In the court ruling, Mr Justice Eady said that, whilst he could refer the matter to the Attorney General, nothing would be achieved by this, as it was sufficient penalty for my behaviour to be mentioned in a public judgement. On top of that, I faced the grim reality that recent events would overshadow the many achievements BP had made since 1995. During my tenure as chief executive, the corporation's market value quintupled. We had grown the business from one of the weaker of the so-called Seven Sisters[3] into a major world player, employing tens of thousands of people from Houston to Moscow to Kuala Lumpur. At one point, BP accounted for £1 in every £6 received in dividends by pension funds in the UK. All of those accomplishments suddenly seemed like footnotes. Editors would spin today's news as a story of power, sex and lies. And in a moment I would have to give them their photograph.

The elevator doors opened. I could see the photographers outside with their lenses pointed and ready to fire. Upstairs my team had been sad and tearful as I prepared to depart. I was deeply grateful to them, but I did not show any emotion and I offered no parting words. I was very focused on getting through the next few moments.

I had one recurring thought, which came from memories of my mother, an Auschwitz survivor, who lived with me for the last fourteen years of her life. Almost all of her family were murdered during the war, and she had lived through a period of intense pain and suffering. But in a way that we might find difficult to comprehend in today's world of emotional expression and candidness, she never dwelled on her past. She never let that dark period diminish her sense of humanity, the knowledge that she too had human rights and that she could face everything standing up straight.

An illuminated green line runs through the lobby of BP and leads to the exit. I followed it into the scrum. One shutter click became a thousand. I paused on the pavement and smiled. What else can you do? Cameramen pushed and shoved, and some attempted to get a rise out of me, which surely would have made for better photographs. Someone shouted the epithet 'gay scum'. As BP security guards cleared a path for me to get into the car, a pushy photographer was shoved to the ground. One of the security guards looked down at him and said, with some irony, 'I'm so sorry.'

Roddy Kennedy, the head of press at BP at the time, accompanied me during the short drive back to my home in Chelsea. Peter, my driver, who had previously worked with the police, had to lose a convoy of motorbikes chasing us with cameras. Amid the commotion, we sat there in silence. It felt as though all the air had been sucked out of the vehicle.

Driving away from the corporation that I helped to build felt like dying. For decades, I dissembled and fenced off a large portion of my life to prevent all of this from happening. I had ducked and weaved and been evasive for as long as I could. But on that day, almost inevitably, my two worlds collided. In the fallout, I lost the job that had structured my entire life.

After all those years of worry and dread, I could not help but think that my fears were finally justified. At that moment, I was convinced that I had been right all along.

GROWING UP

MY REFUSAL EARLIER in my career to acknowledge my sexual orientation publicly stemmed from a lack of confidence. That is not to say that the oil industry had beaten me down. That was far from the reality. Navigating my way from trainee to chief executive had given me faith in my abilities and taught me to project self-assurance, almost to the point of seeming arrogant.

But inside I concealed deep unease and had to deal with inner turmoil almost daily. It is difficult to feel good about yourself when you are embarrassed to show who you actually are. That feeling did not diminish as I rose through the ranks. I grew more scared the more senior I became because I felt I had more to lose.

As with so many gay men and women, my feelings of anxiety began to grow long before I contemplated a career in business: all the conditioning, the questioning and the self-doubt started early.

I attended the King's School Ely, a boarding school in rural Cambridgeshire. Set up in AD 970, it spread out over several monastic buildings and had strong connections with the Cathedral of Ely, where we often worshipped. A liberal Church of England school, there was little talk of hellfire and damnation, and the topic of homosexuality did not feature in any religious lessons that I can remember. There was a conspiracy of silence on the topic; it was as if it did not exist.

Despite popular myth, it is simply not true that, at an all-male boarding school, there was a storm of gay activity. Homosexuality was still illegal as I came of age in the 1960s. We were vaguely aware of that. I never saw any homophobic bullying, and there was not any whispering about students or teachers. Instead, students who had a sexual encounter were quietly expelled. They simply disappeared and no explanation followed. The message was clear: being gay was wrong.

The consequences, inside school and out of it, were clear, but that did not stop sexual desire or activity. I had my first gay experiences overseas when I was a young teenager. My father worked abroad for BP, and I would spend my summers enjoying the sun in a decidedly more relaxed atmosphere than in the UK. I had a few separate encounters with friends of my age. Their parents also worked for oil companies. I never felt guilty, though I did worry that somebody would find out what we had done. Fortunately, I did not need to make a pact with my friends. We followed the same tacit code of silence, one held together by our mutual terror of being found out.

My parents were very worldly wise. They had travelled the world and welcomed people to our home regardless of their ethnic or religious backgrounds. But, as at school, gay people did not feature in any discussions. The script in our family, and I would imagine in many others, did not include room for sexuality, or even more basic questions about whether I had a girlfriend. My father was a typical Englishman of his generation, who neither talked about his feelings nor expected you to talk about yours. He had gone to war for Britain as a captain in the military. The stoicism that got him through carried on after he returned.

My mother had a thousand reasons for avoiding the topic and most of them stemmed from surviving the Holocaust. Born to a Catholic father and a Jewish mother, she grew up in a largely Catholic community in Oradea, Romania. Given the family's ties to Catholicism, she and her five siblings might have escaped. But someone betrayed them and the Nazis put my mother and her family on freight trains to Auschwitz. Upon arrival, she was sent by the Nazis to a part of Auschwitz where she would join other slave labourers in a munitions factory. Several of her relatives were sent to the extermination camp known as Birkenau. She never saw her parents again.

Having witnessed the worst of human nature, she was wary of trusting people. Suspicion clouded much of her thinking. 'Don't trust people with your secrets,' she told me from the time I was a child. It was a lesson I took to heart.

We never discussed what she saw and experienced in Auschwitz. She had locked those memories away and, despite my curiosity, I would never ask her to relive any of the misery. As I grew up and learned more about the war, it later became obvious to me that, buried in her anguish, there must have been memories of gay prisoners who were marked out by wearing pink triangles.

Did she suspect I was gay? I do not know. But I am sure of this: she was a great believer that any sign of weakness was bad. I am certain she would have regarded my homosexuality as a disadvantage that must be hidden away in order to prevent the catastrophic. Periods of crisis turn people into pragmatists. She was one of the most practical people I have ever known. I think if I had disclosed my sexual orientation to her, she would have said, 'I don't care if you're gay or straight. You're going to get married and have children. And keep it to yourself: nothing good will come of it.' I suspect she would have said the same thing regardless of how old I was.

By my late teens, my mother's warnings had made me suspicious of others. Like all young men, I was gripped by a growing awareness of sexual fantasy and desire. Whenever the feelings arose, I thought to myself, 'Do nothing, say nothing.' I was already learning to separate aspects of my life into compartments. I filled one with the stories and the images I needed to make me socially acceptable. I filled the other with the hidden feelings and secret thoughts I could share with no one.

I went on to study physics at Cambridge University, where the divide between my inner and outer life hardened further still. I did not worry about people suspecting I was gay because they did not expect students to have girl-friends. Only a small fraction of the student body was female at the time, and men and women were almost entirely segregated. We lived in separate colleges and ate in different dining rooms.

I joined the Lady Margaret Boat Club as a coxswain on one of the men's crew teams. Anti-gay banter was not commonplace, and the most severe slurs with gay connotations were 'poofter' and 'shirt lifter'. I had the occasional crush and would exchange glances with my fellow rowers in the locker room, but I never dared to take it further. The only gay experience I had then was reading James Baldwin's novel *Giovanni's Room*, the story of a young American man who has an affair with an Italian bartender. Any small connection to gay life was like gold dust.

CAREER

IN 1969, I accepted a job with BP. I wanted to go to the US, and BP decided to send me to Alaska. It was not what I had in mind. But I accepted the offer and started my career in the frozen tundra, above the Arctic Circle, 650 miles north of Anchorage. I learned my trade as a petroleum engineer as part of a team that drilled exploration wells. I was the lowest of the low. It was BP's way of knocking the stuffing out of you so that you did not think too highly of yourself. Over time, my responsibilities grew as I was promoted through various jobs in New York, San Francisco, London and Calgary.

As my career progressed and my hours became longer, I channelled any personal frustration about my identity into my work. I saw absolutely no purpose being served by coming out. My career was going in the right direction and the line between my private and public lives was clear. Inside the office, I did not have any particular sexual profile. Outside it, I had my unseen life as a man who met gay people at bars and occasionally had sexual encounters. These two worlds never came together. I was happy about that. My sensitivity to danger was honed through great practice.

By 1981, I had been with BP for twelve years. I was thirty-three years old when I moved to Aberdeen, the Scottish city known for its granite buildings and extraordinarily rare beautiful summer days. I had been appointed manager of the Forties field, the largest oilfield in the North Sea and one of BP's most important production assets. Twice a month I spent my weekends on our massive offshore platforms. Staff jokingly referred to the dozen platform managers as the 'college of cardinals' and to me as the 'pope'.

One weekend evening when I was onshore, I went into the only gay club in town. I had been to gay venues elsewhere, but this was my first time in Aberdeen. I was absolutely terrified, but I had calculated that the risk of seeing anyone from BP was slim to none. I met someone and we went home together. We did not reveal much personal information about ourselves, but he was clearly an educated professional of some kind. I probably told him my name. When you are called 'John Browne' you might as well be 'John Doe'.

Two days later I was in the office and I saw him walking towards me in a corridor. In a split second, I could feel my temperature rise and scanned the area to make sure no one else could see whatever reaction I was about to have. I had hundreds of people working for me at this point. How many of them would now joke that the pope had sinned?

It was a fleeting moment of monumental internal crisis, but it passed without incident. As it turned out, the man I had met worked for another division of the company. It was obvious that he was in the same situation as I was. Later, on the rare occasions we spotted each other, we acted like complete strangers. It was naive of me to think that I was the only one trying to keep a secret.

Pursuing a long-term relationship never crossed my mind. The practical barriers were simply too high. The corporate ladder is slippery enough on its own. Why complicate your ascent by throwing oil on the rungs? Although I did not know at the time, my boss in New York, the late Frank Rickwood, was gay. Frank was probably not the only gay man in BP. In fact, in the early 1970s, Sir Maurice Bridgeman, chairman of BP from 1960 to 1969, is reported to have said of the marketing department that it was 'full of tired queens'. My close friend Gini Savage remembers that before my time in BP it was known as 'British Pansy', with marketing managers in Japan, Italy, Portugal and Spain forming a sort of gay mafia. The same probably did not apply to the more rugged explorers with whom I worked. By 1981, the AIDS epidemic was fuelling homophobia across the world, bringing with it another reason to suppress any thoughts of a homosexual relationship.[4]

My family situation complicated matters. My father died in 1980 after a long battle with diabetes and a series of amputations resulting from gangrene. My mother was bereft and struggled to make sense of what to do with herself. She lived with me on and off in the early 1980s. By 1986, when I relocated to Cleveland, Ohio, she had moved in with me for good. I now realise that I did not only want to look after my mother. I needed her to look after me and to protect me from my own desires.

The steady success I experienced at BP reinforced my two-track life. I had risen to the post of chief financial officer of the Standard Oil Company of Ohio. I enjoyed my job, and my mother enjoyed travelling with me around the US. Yet I was obviously lonely. I persuaded myself that I could do my job and take care of my mother, while having the occasional thrill of meeting someone – albeit in a very complicated way. Sometimes that meant visiting a bar while on a business trip to New York. Sometimes, in the era before the Internet, that meant responding to a classified ad and arranging a meeting. The longer I kept up my charade, the more successful I became. At times, I found my double life very thrilling and I thought that conducting it somehow improved my skill at sensing danger, as if I were a spy in training. I persuaded myself that this was the right way to live.

After becoming chief executive, I regarded personal discretion as vital to the company's interests. I became more reserved and less willing to seek out companionship. We were transforming BP into a global giant. I had regular dealings with business and political leaders in a number of socially conservative countries. I was worried that any disclosure would damage business relationships, particularly those in the Middle East, in some countries of which homosexuality is still punishable by death. I believed that keeping my professional and personal worlds separate was better for each of them.

I am sure now that some people knew, or strongly suspected, that I was gay. A grown man bringing his mother to company events would have caused sniggering. But I was far too busy to get wind of the gossip in the coffee room or around the water cooler.

Fortunately, my mother was well liked by everyone. She played the role of hostess with aplomb, and became part of the theatre and tradition of BP events and dinners. She was an unpaid member of the company payroll. On the occasions she was not there, people would ask, 'Where is Paula?' She was one of the more interesting people they were likely to encounter during an evening, not just because of her background but also because of her presence.

She was vivacious, intelligent and fashionable. Women admired her jewellery and dress sense, and she grew more elegant with time. It is not an exaggeration to say that she was a huge asset professionally. On a personal level, she had also become a surrogate partner.

My mother fell ill a couple of months after enjoying a superb millennium celebration at Cliveden House, the former home of the Astors. I was with her when she died on 9 July 2000. We had a nurse at home around the clock. She put my mother on a tiny amount of morphine just to keep her pain away. One Sunday we had brought the newspapers to her, but she sat there reading and said, 'I can't read the newspaper.' And then she was dead.

In the months that followed, I was desperately lonely. If I were heterosexual, I would have been married and had children, and we would have all mourned together. But I had no family to mourn with, and my loneliness sapped all my energy and strength.

I do not remember precisely when, but a year or more after my mother's death I began actively looking for a partner. I had no experience in doing this. Today's young people do not flinch at the thought of turning to the Internet. But the Internet was not what it is today, and for someone of my generation, the experience was cloaked in shame, which made it all the more intimidating. My quest for a partner led predictably to disaster.

COMING DOWN

ON THE NIGHT of 1 May 2007, I slept very deeply. I was physically exhausted from months of personal and professional upheaval. For weeks, I had been smoking rather than eating, and my weight had dropped to 58 kilograms, too light for a man approaching sixty, even one of my short stature. I was mentally drained. It takes a lot of intellectual muscle to hold yourself up when the ground is shifting beneath you.

On 3 May, just two days after my resignation, I was scheduled to deliver a speech in Brussels as part of the Amartya Sen Lecture Series on sustainable development. The invitation, received months earlier, was a great honour. I worried that the deluge of press coverage would distract attention from the lecture and its purpose.

My friends and colleagues had encouraged me to avoid any and all newspapers. But surely the invited audience of diplomats and academics would not have escaped the lurid headlines: 'HUBRIS, LIES AND THE GAY AFFAIR THAT BROUGHT DOWN BP BOSS', 'BIG PORKIES: OIL BOSS LOSES £15M PAY-OFF', 'LORD BROWNE: THE SUN KING WHO LOST HIS SHINE'. Some would have read the harsh commentary published in tabloids such as the *Daily Mail*. 'How close he came to being remembered and revered as one of the greats,' it said. 'How much he yearned for it. But the truth reared up yesterday to expose the top-to-toe impeccability of Lord Browne of Madingley, group chief executive of BP, as a hubristic sham.'[5] *The Guardian*'s comment was: 'It is a coincidence that a man seen as a moderniser in the business world should ultimately fall in such an old-fashioned way. In his support one fund manager in the City described his need to depart last night as "outrageous" but the man who lived professionally by risk had effectively been slain in the same way.'[6]

I suggested that I might not come, but the organisers insisted that recent events were irrelevant to them, and so I went to Belgium. The speech was decidedly optimistic, arguing that a successful transition to a lower-carbon world is eminently possible. I recognised that the pace of change was critical, but concluded that we could move quickly enough to avert the serious risks that the scientists had started to identify. In short, I believed that a shared danger created a shared purpose.

The standing ovation was invigorating, and a reminder that I still had a platform even if I did not have the title of chief executive. Some hostility punctuated the applause. 'Lord Browne, are you looking forward to going to jail?' an English journalist from *The Daily Telegraph* asked. 'You lied. You must answer. This is a matter of public interest.' The audience booed him and he promptly returned to his seat. Between their standing ovation and his pointed comment, I was very confused about who was thinking what.

I had no illusions: there were certainly people who could not stand me, whether because of my sexuality or other perceived shortcomings or flaws. I am sure there were plenty of people who loved seeing me stumble so publicly. I just had to ignore them. The incident in Brussels weakened me, though I understood that the journalist was simply doing his job. I was not a person to him. I was a news story. Running a public company had taught me to appreciate the difference. My lesson from that day was that there is great power in speaking out at a time when people least expect it.

Oscar Wilde once wrote that every saint has a past and every sinner has a future. I began to see that in the days and weeks that followed my resignation. A large number of my friends signed an open letter of support published in the UK press. BP insisted that I keep my office for as long as I needed it. That proved to be very useful as thousands of letters poured in from around the world. All but one of the letters was supportive, and each buoyed me in some way. They came from friends and former colleagues, business people, politicians, artists and engineers. They offered help and advice. They reminded me of times we had spent together or things we had achieved. A broadcast journalist actually wrote to warn me that his office would be sending an interview request. He added a request of his own: 'Please make sure you refuse.'

My resignation served as a channel for even the most reserved and private people to express their thoughts, sympathy and outrage. For days, I did nothing other than read their letters and reply: emails with emails, handwritten letters with handwritten letters. My assistant had to use an assistant to help her sort through the growing mountain of correspondence. At one point, someone in the office said rather flippantly that the experience was like being able to read your own obituary. She had a point. People had written such nice things.

At least a third of the letters came from complete strangers, many of whom shared deeply personal tragedies that stemmed from being gay or lesbian. Some had been exposed by newspapers and forced to come out. Others had been charged with criminal offences and imprisoned. Still others had to divorce, leave the country or sell their house. Whether they came from Russia or Spain, France or the US, each of these people told an extraordinary tale of human suffering.

In a court adjudicated by the tabloids, these men and women had been deemed guilty. But all they were 'guilty' of was being gay, made worse by newspapers preying on their vulnerability. In the aftermath, some of them had survived and gone on to thrive. Others had simply collapsed.

I found their honesty inspiring. On one level, it was comforting that people were thinking of me. On another, it was uplifting to know that I was not unique in being outed. It helped me feel like less of an oddity. My situation had a high profile and was painful, but it was not unusual.

STARTING AGAIN

I PUT ON a brave face as I left BP, but in reality my resignation hurt me deeply. The pain took months to subside. Under normal circumstances I would not have chosen to exit so abruptly. But it was the right decision. The last thing I wanted to do was tarnish BP's reputation by lingering on in my position, or even in the building. After a few days of using my old office, I packed my things and left without saying goodbye.

I knew that I needed to create a new life. As a starting point, I resolved to resign from a series of positions. The manner in which I had been outed simply would not reflect well on the companies and organisations I advised, so I would spare them the trouble of having to push me. I wrote to Goldman Sachs, on whose board of directors I sat, offering my resignation. They accepted it without comment. Lee Scott, then CEO of Walmart, rang me with sadness in his voice to withdraw an informal offer to join their board of directors. He said the situation was untenable, given the active religious Right in Arkansas. I went to see the chief executive of Apax Partners, the London-based private equity firm, to say that I would be stepping down as chairman. Much to my surprise, he replied that I should stay on. I offered to step down as president of the Royal Academy of Engineering. They would not hear of it.

My secret fear that life would end after BP started to seem overly dramatic. For me, the events surrounding 1 May were clinically traumatic, but to the outside world, they were mere items in the evening news. As with the protagonists of so many other scandals, I was yesterday's news within two weeks. By then the photographers had stopped doorstepping me and following me to dinner. At the end of May, I visited some close friends at their farm in Spain. We took walks, looked at wild flowers and over the course of several days they took every opportunity to remind me of one of their favourite aphorisms: 'The dogs bark, but the caravan moves on.'

Other people my age had partners with whom they could talk. Perhaps a monk can work out problems in prayer and in solitude, but I needed outside help to recognise myself, and I relied on friends and others for this.

One of them put me at ease early on by quoting Aldous Huxley, who apparently said that 'the higher the brow, the lower the trousers'. They gently guided me to understand and enjoy the new context of my life: being out and being outed. Events happen and the context changes, but I was still essentially the same person, only wiser. I had been through great upheaval, and I had survived and learned a lot, about people, about my friends and about myself. I had rid myself of the shame.

They encouraged me to do what I was good at. That is how you make a contribution. I had proven myself at BP. It was time to get on and do business again.

I had little desire to pursue the position of chairman or chief executive at another FTSE 100 company. Returning to the public markets would mean returning to the limelight. I was also realistic. To a headhunter I would have been seen as 'controversial', too hot to handle after being forced into a corner and lying, resigning from BP and coming out of the closet at the same time. Private business would be the way forward. I became a partner at Riverstone, a private equity firm specialising in energy. The drama surrounding my resignation did not seem to matter to my new US partners. They simply wanted to clarify whether I was the subject of any related litigation; I was not.

Sadly, there were some people, mostly from the business world, who never again displayed any warmth to me.

Perhaps they felt I no longer had business to give or patronage to dispense. For the vast majority of people, however, my coming out was a non-event. Given the dramatic circumstances, they cared about my well-being. Some of them had long suspected I was gay, so the news did not come as a shock. For others, the events simply added a new dimension to the same old person.

People who have slightly imperfect vision do not often realise it. It is only when they have an eye test and slip on a new pair of spectacles that they realise what they have been missing. It took a while for me to feel lighter. But as the months went by, it was as if I had unhooked myself from a gigantic ball and chain. I became less reserved and more open. I felt much more relaxed with myself; life is easier when lived out in the open. I kept thinking about what my mother would have thought about everything that had happened. She would have said, I am sure, that disasters should never spell an end, only a beginning. And I think she would have liked my more relaxed self.

Of the thousands of letters that I received in the month after I resigned, only one was delivered to my home address. This intrigued me. It came from a thirty-two-year-old man named Nghi. He was born in Saigon to a Vietnamese mother and a Chinese father, and grew up in Germany. He had followed the news coverage of my outing while travelling in New Zealand before starting a new job with the same investment bank from which I had resigned as board member only a few weeks earlier. He had seen a photograph of my house in one of the newspapers, which helped him deduce my address. Not exactly intending to start a new relationship when embarking on a new job, he was nonetheless curious about a man he had known little about but whose story had even reached the headlines of newspapers as far away as the Bay of Islands, the northern tip of New Zealand. It was remarkable. We met for a drink on 1 June 2007, one month after I had resigned from BP, and we have been together ever since.

To help me relax, I had a cigar during the evening of our first meeting. It was to be my last. After twenty-seven years of enjoying three to four cigars a day, I suddenly had no desire to continue. Stopping cold turkey was no easy feat. Soon afterwards, I began regular fitness sessions with a personal trainer. After six months, I felt as though I was living in a rejuvenated body. This boost to my physical welfare was one of the surprising results of my outing. It would not have happened otherwise.

REFLECTION

SOME TIME AFTER my resignation from BP, while making an inventory of my library, I came across a copy of Cavafy's poems. Arguably the most influential Greek poet of the last century, Cavafy dealt with his own homosexuality in many poems with titles such as 'The Bandaged Shoulder' and 'One Night'. Lyrical and accessible, they come wrapped in pain and anxiety, and hint at the psychological exile of a gay man in a straight world. I would read them often as a twenty-something young man in New York, when I was still in the foothills of my career. I particularly remember the fourteen-line poem 'Hidden Things', in which Cavafy talks of the barrier that separated him from all the people around him. I always imagined that barrier as sheaths of glass, surrounding him on every side.

When I opened a book of his poems all those years later, I found that I had written out the translation of that poem by hand on the inside cover, along with the date: 25 August 1973. I would have been twenty-five years old.

HIDDEN THINGS[7]

From all the things I did and all the things I said
let no one try to find out who I was.
An obstacle was there transforming
the actions and the manner of my life.
An obstacle was often there
to silence me when I began to speak.
From my most unnoticed actions
and my most veiled writing—
from these alone will I be understood.
But maybe it isn't worth so much concern
and so much effort to discover who I really am.
Later, in a more perfect society,
someone else made just like me
is certain to appear and act freely.

There is still much work to be done. But forty years after I first read it, this poem seems less like the wish of a young man, and more like a premonition.

CHAPTER TWO

BEAUTY AND BIGOTRY

THE KEEPER OF Greek and Roman antiquities unveiled a piece of silverwork depicting two pairs of male lovers. I wanted to sink into the ground.

From 1995 to 2005, I served as a trustee of the British Museum. My fellow trustees included distinguished people from all walks of life with a shared passion for art and antiquities. Many of them could speak with authority on different objects in the collection and how each of them fitted into human civilisation. We convened almost every month on a Saturday morning to review the museum's strategy, performance and fund-raising efforts. We also decided on which objects the museum should purchase for its permanent collection. In order to help us do that, each keeper, commonly known as a curator elsewhere, would display favoured objects at a 'bazaar' before each meeting.

One morning in 1999, the curators were particularly taken with an object called the Warren Cup, a small ornate silver goblet. It was thought to have been made about 2,000 years ago, and was said to have been unearthed near Jerusalem.[1] Bandits and invading armies sometimes melted down silver objects from this period, but this extraordinary example of Roman craftsmanship survived. One side of the cup depicts two pairs of male lovers performing sexual intercourse with a lyre resting in the background, suggesting that musicians had helped create a romantic atmosphere.

A slave can be seen peeping through a door that has been left ajar.

The trustees debated the provenance and authenticity of the cup, while particularly admiring the craftsmanship of the repoussé work (images beaten into the silver from the inside to the outside). The keeper explained how it would have been the centrepiece of private parties for a wealthy family and that Romans would have viewed it as an object of exquisite beauty, not as pornography. It was a truly enticing masterpiece with an extraordinary history. Yet I could not bring myself to speak in favour of the object because of its homosexual imagery. I thought that praising the work would be tantamount to coming out of the closet. Despite the cup being only 11 centimetres tall, for me it cast a very long shadow.

Ultimately, the trustees endorsed the purchase of the cup for £1.8 million, making it then the most expensive acquisition in the history of the museum.[2] Setting aside my own discomfort, that purchase demonstrated the broader shift in attitudes towards homosexuality that had taken place in the preceding decades. In the 1950s, when homosexual acts were still illegal in the UK, the British Museum actually turned down an opportunity to purchase the cup. So did the Fitzwilliam Museum at the University of Cambridge. In 1953, a customs official in the US denied the Warren Cup entry to the country because of its explicit imagery.[3]

Almost fifty years later, the British had moved beyond that prudishness, at least in the liberally minded corridors of the British Museum. The Warren Cup has been on display ever since its purchase, and for a time the museum even sold replicas in its gift shop for £250.

'It's not just a superb piece of Roman imperial metalwork,' Neil MacGregor, the museum's director, writes. 'From party cup to scandalous vessel and finally to an iconic museum piece, this object reminds us that the way societies view sexual relationships is never fixed.'[4]

The British Museum was to prove this again when they mounted an exhibition about Hadrian and his times in 2008. Most people in the UK associate this Roman emperor with the building of a wall that separates England from Scotland. What is of less common knowledge is Hadrian's sexual taste. He had a male lover, Antinous, who was with him for several years. Antinous drowned mysteriously in the Nile; some say it was because he became inconvenient to the emperor. After his death, he was venerated in sculpture. Temples were built in his honour, his name was given to cities and he became a god. The exhibition served to remind us that homosexual love was not regarded as unusual in Roman times.

In 1976, towards the end of my four-year stint in New York, an observant French female friend gave me a copy of Marguerite Yourcenar's 1951 book *Memoirs of Hadrian*. In this series of fictional letters written close to his death, Hadrian refers to his long-lost lover with a passion that came from 'the hardest and most condensed form of ardour, the grain of gold pulled from the fire, not from the ashes'.[5] He declares that the extended peace during his reign stemmed from his relationship with his young paramour. The book is filled with beauty and tenderness, but I read it with a sense of guilt. My friend had identified something in me that I was not ready to share.

Thirty-two years later, on my sixtieth birthday, another friend gave me a first edition of Yourcenar's book. At that point I had been out of the closet for nine months. My attitude towards the book reflected an evolving attitude towards myself. I now read it without any sense of shame. I saw the book, and the love shared by Hadrian and Antinous, for what it was: a gift.

MILLENNIA BEFORE OSCAR Wilde's lover Lord Alfred Douglas described homosexuality as 'the Love that dare not speak its name', ancient civilisations worshipped gods who engaged in sexual activity with deities and mortals of the same sex. From India to Rome, these gods gave little thought to the gender of their lovers. They embraced homosexual dalliances as often did their followers. At various times and in various cultures, societies have tolerated, and even celebrated, sexual acts between two men and between two women.

The Greeks believed that sexual desire could overwhelm the gods just as it overwhelmed humans. Robert Aldrich, an Australian historian, notes that: 'In this respect, Greek mythology functioned as a mirror upon which Greek men could project their sexual desires and wherein they could recognise themselves.'[6]

That mirror allowed them to see all manner of sexual relations. Apollo, the god of the sun, fathered several children with female deities. But he also boasted an extensive list of male lovers including Hyacinth, an athletic Spartan prince. One day, while Apollo was throwing the discus, Zephyrus, the male god of the west wind, grew jealous of their romance and blew the discus off course, killing Hyacinth. His blood gave rise to the flower that now bears his name.[7] Plutarch wrote that Heracles, the strongest mortal and an embodiment of virility, had so many male lovers that it would be impossible to list all of them.[8] And Poseidon, god of the sea, raped the male god Tantalus.[9]

Not even Zeus, the supreme ruler of the gods, could resist the beauty of Ganymede, the most beautiful male mortal in Troy. In one telling of the story, Zeus, disguised as an eagle, abducts Ganymede and compels the youth to serve as his cupbearer. Ganymede spends his nights in his master's bed, and the days intoxicating him with wine. Sophocles wrote that the mortal had mastered the art of 'setting Zeus's power aflame with his thighs'.[10]

BLAME

TALES OF LOVE and devotion eventually gave way to actions of exclusion and cruelty. The interpretation of the words of Leviticus[11] has led to extraordinary repression and persecution of gay people, all in the name of pious devotion to a god. A permissive attitude towards homosexual acts was thought to have disastrous consequences; the destruction of Sodom was popularly put down to the prevalence of homosexual activity. That was, however, only the beginning: leaders and religious figures later attributed other catastrophic events to homosexual behaviour. In AD 538, Rome's Christian Emperor Justinian I issued an edict calling for the execution of those engaging in gay sexual acts, whose sexual exploits were at the root of 'famines, earthquakes and pestilences'.[12] Following the bubonic plague, which wiped out at least a third of Europe's population, Jews were blamed for spreading the disease, except in communities where they were absent. In those places, homosexuals and prostitutes absorbed the public's wrath.[13]

Across Europe, the bubonic plague fostered an outburst of homophobia;[14] this was to be seen again at the outbreak of AIDS. The reaction to the plague was particularly pronounced in Italian cities, which non-Italians ridiculed for allegedly having the highest population of homosexuals in the world.[15] In both Venice and Florence, public bodies were set up to eradicate anyone who engaged in gay sex, for fear that they might recruit young men into their ranks.[16] The public was encouraged to inform on homosexuals, whom officials would then torture to extract confessions. 'The convicted sodomite could then be displayed in the pillory, to be abused and beaten by righteous citizens,' writes historian Byrne Fone. 'If he survived this ordeal he was, at last, burned at the stake.'[17] In other instances, the accused was first publicly castrated.

Homosexual acts became a crime throughout Europe, frequently punishable by death. By the seventeenth century, laws that criminalised same-sex relations had been promulgated in France, Spain, England, Prussia and Denmark. In the Netherlands, a total of seventy-five alleged homosexuals were executed in 1730 alone and over the next eighty years nearly one thousand trials were held.[18]

But from the late seventeenth century, freedoms afforded to gay men began to expand, particularly in France. Enlightenment thinkers, driven by concerns for privacy and secularism, did not couch sexual acts between men in religious terms.[19] They argued that it was not a crime because, assuming both parties consented, it did not violate anyone's rights. France's Constituent Assembly agreed, and by 1791 homosexuality was no longer a crime.[20] In the nineteenth century, a distinct gay subculture began to form. Urbanisation brought gay people together in cities from Paris to Amsterdam to London.[21] Men explored their sexuality in parks, public squares, public lavatories, railway stations and shopping arcades.[22]

The Yokel's Preceptor, a London publication from 1855, warned tourists of gay debauchery in these terms: 'The increase of these monsters in the shape of men, commonly designated margeries, poofs, etc., of late years, in the great Metropolis, renders it necessary for the safety of the public that they should be made known … that these monsters actually walk the street the same as the whores, looking out for a chance!'[23]

By 1861, England and Wales had abolished the death penalty for buggery, but it still carried a sentence that ranged from ten years to life imprisonment. As the British Empire grew, its leaders felt a need to 'civilise' its colonies and correct 'native' customs, which included homosexual acts.[24] In 1860, administrators drafted a penal code in India that criminalised gay sex, or, as it read, 'carnal intercourse against the order of nature'. They subsequently installed variations of that code in British colonies from Fiji to Zambia.[25] The UK decriminal-ised sex between men in 1967, but the majority of its former colonies and protectorates have not followed that example. At the end of 2013, forty-four of these countries still had anti-homosexuality laws in place.[26]

BIGOTRY

MY MOTHER FREQUENTLY told me that she could divide her life into three distinct periods: the time before the Second World War; the time she spent with my father, whom she met after the war; and the years she spent with me following my father's death. There was one gap. She blacked out her year at Auschwitz. Her mental fortitude and steely determination carried her through that hell. Once she was free, she drew on those same qualities to bury her memories in the past.

Two experiences helped me understand why she approached her past in this way. Towards the end of her life, we visited the United States Holocaust Memorial Museum in Washington DC. More than one million people visit the museum every year.[27] But there was an eerie silence as we walked past reproductions of gas chambers, and read stories of people who had died in concentration camps. Displays showed the everyday items, including saucepans and suitcases, that people had packed with them before being loaded on to the trains to death camps. My mother wanted to stop at a particular display that contained a collection of shoes. She told me that the five-year-old daughter of her sister, my cousin, had been sent to the gas chamber. One would have expected me to console my mother. When we left she had to console me.

In the 1980s, we travelled to Auschwitz, which I visited again in June 2013. On both occasions I was reminded of the scale and systematic organisation of the killing. There is no doubt that Jews were the overwhelming target of the Nazis. But display cases capture the cruel efficiency of classification, and the sustained persecution of minority groups. Yellow stars signified Jewish prisoners. Black triangles marked those of Roma descent. Purple triangles were assigned to Jehovah's Witnesses. Pink triangles were reserved for homosexuals.

During the Third Reich, authorities arrested approximately 100,000 suspected homosexuals, and imprisoned half of them.[28] Between 1934 and 1941, officials castrated more than 2,000 sex offenders, which included rapists, paedophiles and a large number of homosexuals.[29] Doctors did not hesitate to conduct the procedures. As historian Geoffrey Giles writes, one hospital in a Berlin prison completed 111 castrations in the first nine months of 1934: 'The prison doctor proudly reported that he had perfected his technique to the point of completing the entire operation, with only a local anaesthetic, in eight minutes flat. He pronounced it "without a doubt the cheapest method of safeguarding" the community.'[30] In addition, the Nazis sent up to 15,000 gay men to concentration camps.[31] Guards frequently gave gay prisoners the more difficult work assignments, which may explain why they demonstrated a higher death rate, and a lower survival rate after being liberated from the camps.[32] Conditions were so brutal that less than 40 per cent of homosexuals are estimated to have survived.[33] As in past history, lesbians were not regarded as a social or political threat.

Following the war, the Jewish community led efforts to ensure that the world remember the atrocities that had taken place. The Holocaust was an event that deeply scarred the Jewish population more than any other segment of society; many of my own family were murdered. But gay men could not ask for remembrance. Laws that criminalised homosexuality remained in place until 1969 and some men who had survived the concentration camps were re-arrested after the war.[34] Unlike other survivors, homosexuals did not receive reparations after the war;[35] in Germany, compensation for homosexual victims only became available in 2001,[36] by which point most survivors had died. The gay men who died in or survived the concentration camps were not forgotten victims; they had been ignored.

Hitler's regime was not alone in its efforts to eradicate homosexuality during the twentieth century. Doctors in Denmark, West Germany, Norway, Sweden and the US performed thousands of lobotomies on gay patients.[37] Recently revealed military files show that during and after the Second World War, the US government forced veterans who it deemed mentally ill, including schizophrenics, psychotics and homosexuals, to undergo the procedure.[38] Electro-shock therapy also became popular as a way of 'curing' homosexuals. In 1935, a professor from New York University instructed clinicians at a meeting of the American Psychological Association that the therapy would only work if they administered shocks at 'intensities considerably higher than those usually employed on human subjects'.[39] In 1952, the American Psychiatric Association published a manual that first classified homosexuality as a 'sociopathic personality disturbance'.[40]

Defining homosexuality as a mental illness further reinforced negative stereotypes of gay men and women, and implicitly justified anti-gay prejudice. A 1950 Congressional report entitled *Employment of Homosexuals and Other Sex Perverts in Government* spelled out the reasons why the US government should not hire gay employees. 'It is generally believed that those who engage in overt acts of perversion lack the emotional stability of normal persons,' it said. 'In addition there is an abundance of evidence to sustain the conclusion that indulgence in acts of sex perversion weakens the moral fiber of an individual to a degree that he is not suitable for a position of responsibility.'[41] The report helped start the so-called 'Lavender Scare'. Officials believed that Communist infiltrators could get classified information from gay staff by threatening to expose them. By 1953, President Dwight Eisenhower's Executive Order 10450 had established 'sexual perversion' as grounds for dismissing federal employees.[42]

Those who were dismissed would find little solace at the bar. Police regularly raided gay establishments and arrested the patrons on the grounds of public indecency. In the 1950s, California briefly allowed its Department of Alcoholic Beverages Control to revoke the licence of any establishment that acted as a 'resort ... for sexual perverts'.[43] An essay published in a 1966 edition of *Time*, the country's highest-circulation news magazine, conveys the popular view of gay men. Entitled 'The Homosexual in America', it refers to the gay man as a 'deviate' throughout and states that 'a vast majority of people retain a deep loathing toward him'. It concludes that homosexuality 'deserves no encouragement, no glamorization, no rationalization, no fake status as minority martyrdom, no sophistry about simple differences in taste—and, above all, no pretence that it is anything but a pernicious sickness'.[44] At the time of the article's publication, only one of the fifty states, Illinois, had repealed its homosexuality laws.

Things were no better in the UK of the 1950s and 1960s. In 1954, Alan Turing, the father of the computer, committed suicide having been chemically treated to cure him of homosexuality. In 1955, the eminent lawyer Lord Hailsham railed against homosexuality, calling it a moral and social issue equivalent to drug addiction. It was, he said, a trait induced in the young while they were still impressionable by older gay people. His writings then go on to explain the unnatural use of the bodily organs in activities for which they were not designed.[45] Hailsham became the most senior judge in the land later in his life.

In 1957, Sir John Wolfenden, an academic who eventually became director of the British Museum, published the findings of his inquiry into homosexual offences and prostitution. This proposed that homosexual activity between consenting adult men no longer be criminal. It also proposed toughening up penalties for prostitution.[46] The latter proposal was passed into law within two years, but it took a further eight years for the section on homosexuality to come into law.

During the early 1960s, homophobia, encouraged by prudishness, lack of understanding by the public and a self-righteous judiciary and press, was rife. Many scandals were based on or even 'spiced up' with a suggestion of gay activity, sometimes with an overlay of espionage in an era frightened of the Communist menace. The names of those involved are fading: Vassall, Galbraith, Lord Montagu and Pitt-Rivers, to name a few. Eventually, the recommendations of the

Wolfenden report became law in 1967, during my second year at Cambridge. Changing the law was important, but attitudes took much longer to catch up. E. M. Forster, the great novelist and author of a gay romance, *Maurice*, which he wrote and revised between 1913 and 1960, summed up these attitudes. He attached a note to the manuscript that read, 'Publishable, but worth it?'[47] The book was published in 1971, only after his death the previous year.

Against that backdrop, it is not a surprise that gay life frequently went underground. Anonymous sexual encounters were seen as a necessary compromise. Men craved intimacy with each other, but revealing one's identity could only lead to grave consequences. In the early 1970s, at places like the Continental Baths, a gay bathhouse that had opened in the basement of New York's Ansonia Hotel in 1968, good-looking young men paraded around in towels, sipped cocktails and frequently ended up having sex with complete strangers. To anyone not involved, this appears sleazy. For those lounging by the fountains and dance floor, it would have felt rebellious and liberating. Saunas, bars and clubs were places where they could forget the repression outside. They were also the only places where gay men could socialise among themselves, and the Continental Baths were not merely about sex. Amid all the cruising, it was the venue at which the then completely unknown Bette Midler, accompanied by Barry Manilow on the piano, performed at the side of the pool to rapturous applause. One of my friends, the author Brian Masters, remembers his trips there in glowing terms: 'What wild extravagant freedom after years of being imprisoned in broad daylight!'[48]

By the late 1960s, raids on gay bars in New York City seemed to follow a script. Lights would go out. Police would line up patrons. They would arrest any man without an identification document and also those dressed as women. The raids normally went off without incident, but on 28 June 1969, things did not go according to plan. Perhaps because of years of hostility directed at them, patrons at the Stonewall Inn in Greenwich Village did not cooperate and resisted. Men refused to show their identification documents, and drag queens would not go with female officers to the toilets so as to verify their gender. Those released by police did not scurry home, but instead gathered outside where a mob of onlookers had formed.

Journalist David Carter recounts how police aggression fuelled the crowd's dissent. 'The first hostile act outside the club occurred when a police officer shoved one of the transvestites, who turned and smacked the officer over the head with her purse,' he writes. 'The cop clubbed her, and a wave of anger passed through the crowd, which immediately showered the police with boos and catcalls, followed by a cry to turn the paddy wagon over.'[49]

The crowd outnumbered the police by at least 500. People hurled bottles, bricks and garbage cans at the bar. They trapped the police inside for at least forty-five minutes before reinforcements arrived. Activists daubed the outside of the building with phrases like 'Support gay power' and 'They invaded our rights'. The riots made headlines in all the major newspapers. The following week *The Village Voice* sparked outrage when it ran a story replete with homophobic slurs, mentioning the rioters' 'limp wrists' and the 'forces of faggotry.'[50] A thousand demonstrators gathered outside the newspaper's offices. Looting and street battles ensued in which the gay community sent a clear message about oppression. The *East Village Other*, an underground newspaper in New York, summed up the mounting rage in these terms: 'When did you ever see a fag fight back? ... Now times were a-changin' ... the theme was, "This shit has got to stop!"'[51]

In the years that followed, gay men and women became more visible in society, both in the US and the UK. A growing number of new LGBT publications appeared, including *Gay Flames* in the US and *Gay Times* in the UK.

As a closeted young man, I never wandered into gay bookshops, nor did I seek out gay periodicals. But, as I recently learned, even I have a connection to a revolutionary magazine.

In the summer of 2013, I flew to San Francisco for a business meeting. While I was there I was invited to a performance at the San Francisco Opera by Michael Savage, a former BP executive whom I have known since the early 1970s, and his wife Gini, who is a yoga instructor and poet. I asked her to read an early draft of this book. She agreed and, during our subsequent conversations, it emerged that she had once used a nom de plume, Ruan Bone, to protect her identity as editor of *Lunch*, a 1970s magazine about homosexual life in the UK. I have known her for thirty-five years, but had never before discovered her close link to this early subculture. When you are in the closet, you do not ask questions that might expose yourself or the other person.

In 1972, she wrote in a remarkable editor's column that 'it seems to us that homosexual experience in Britain has changed a great deal over the last 40 years or so … it still has a long way to go … but the exact nature of that experience is still very largely unresearched. We know very little about ourselves, so that it's not surprising sometimes that outsiders have crude or out-of-date ideas about us.'[52] This could have been written in 2012, another forty years on.

Humorous features in the magazine sent up stereotypes about gay people. In an article called 'Spot the Poofter', the author explained that 'poofters like to touch you, to take your arm, to lay a hand on your shoulder. And, as all the world knows, poofters can't whistle!'[53] Lesbians, it advises, smoke pipes. Most importantly, though, *Lunch* interviewed gay role models, including my own hero David Hockney. When asked how he felt about the gay scene, he responded in terms that captured the spirit of change post-Stonewall. 'I'm not sure I know much about the gay scene in England,' he said at the time. 'I feel one should stand up and be counted and do one's bit occasionally though.'[54]

Activists groups like the Gay Activists Alliance, Radicalesbians and Gay Liberation Front put militancy at the heart of their activity,[55] while less radical activists lobbied legislators, professional groups and the media.[56] In 1973, the American Psychiatric Association reversed its position of two decades earlier and declassified homosexuality from being a mental illness.[57] The US Civil Service Commission subsequently removed its ban on hiring homosexuals as federal employees.[58] In 1977, Harvey Milk was elected to the San Francisco Board of Supervisors, becoming the first openly gay elected public official in California. Raids on gay venues diminished and that helped nurture demand for new places for gay people to meet. Historian Domenico Rizzo describes the late 1970s as 'a golden age of bars, nightclubs and baths … when a liberated sexuality seemed to manifest itself in everything from pornography to pop music culture, turning a song like the Village People's 1978 "YMCA" into not only an international hit but also an anthem for a generation'.[59]

The AIDS crisis promptly stopped the music.

TELEVISION

THAT 'GOLDEN AGE' created an image of sleaze and irresponsibility that came to define the reputation of the gay community. Combined with the fears created by AIDS, gay people became portrayed in the mass media as unsavoury and untouchable. That image started to change thanks to the influence of television and movies.

British television began affecting people's attitudes decades ago. In 1986, as public fears over the AIDS crisis continued to mount, the BBC introduced two gay characters into its flagship soap opera *EastEnders*. That year, one character, a middle-class graphic designer, moved to London's East End and began a relationship with a young barrow boy. As the weeks passed, producers treated the characters sympathetically, and exposed the bigotry that the pair had faced from neighbours. In one scene, the local gossip Dot Cotton erupts into a fit of rage when the gay boy reveals his same-sex romance to her, saying, 'I can't clean your flat because it'd be tantamount to condoning it, wouldn't it? Not to mention the two of you may well have AIDS.' She says that God is 'fed up' and 'sent this dreadful plague down' to teach gay men a lesson.[60]

Dot conveyed society's preoccupation with the sex practices of gay people and the habit of linking their lifestyle to AIDS. The scriptwriters at *EastEnders* wanted to move beyond that. They cast their gay characters in an ordinary light, taking them out of the bedrooms and hospital rooms and into cafés, grocery shops and homes. They did so in the face of mounting outrage. In 1987, they showed, for the first time, two gay men kissing. Members of Parliament tabled questions asking whether gay men should be portrayed so sympathetically with the AIDS epidemic raging. One tabloid published an article called 'FILTH! GET THIS OFF OUR SCREENS'.[61] Another ran the headline 'EASTBENDERS!'[62] That same tabloid later described a tender moment between the characters as a 'homosexual love scene between two yuppie poofs'.[63] Two bricks were thrown through a window of the house of Michael Cashman, one of the actors involved. His partner in real life was outed as gay.

'We stood our ground,' Cashman says. 'We moved everything on, and politics and even the tabloids eventually followed.'[64] The new breed of television characters suggested gay life was not all dancing, drugs and disease.

Until the late 1990s, gay characters appeared on US television almost exclusively in minor roles. It was not until Ellen DeGeneres that a lesbian took centre stage in prime time. In April 1997, the comedienne and star of her eponymous sitcom came out in real life, appearing on the cover of *Time* magazine with the headline, 'YEP, I'M GAY'. A few weeks later, 42 million viewers tuned in to watch her television character come out to a therapist played by Oprah Winfrey.[65]

DeGeneres believed that coming out in real life, and on the show, would help paint a fuller picture of the gay community. 'I did it selfishly for myself and because I thought it was a great thing for the show, which desperately needed a point of view,' she said in the interview in which she came out. 'If other people come out that's fine. I mean, it would be great if for no other reason than just to show the diversity, so it's not just the extremes. Because unfortunately those are the people who get the most attention on the news. You know, when you see the parades and you see dykes on bikes or these men dressed as women. I don't want to judge them. I don't want to come off like I'm attacking them—the whole point of what I'm doing is acceptance of everybody's differences. It's just that I don't want them representing the entire gay community, and I'm sure they don't want me representing them. We're individuals.'[66]

Ratings suggested that viewers wanted to see those differences. Shortly after this episode, *The Economist* ran an article arguing that 'if homosexuality were a choice, now would be a great time to choose it'.[67] NBC launched *Will & Grace*, a sitcom with two gay lead characters. From 2001 until 2005, its rating was the second highest in the US.[68]

In 2012, the percentage of LGBT characters in prime-time television drama on the five US broadcast networks grew to an all-time high. In 2007, only 1.1 per cent of all characters were lesbian, gay, bisexual or transgender, but by 2012 it had climbed to 4.4 per cent.[69] According to Herndon Graddick, the former president of GLAAD,[70] that 'reflects a cultural change in the way gay and lesbian people are seen in our society. More and more Americans have come to accept their LGBT family members, friends, co-workers, and peers, and as audiences tune into their favorite programs, they expect to see the same diversity of people they encounter in their daily lives.'[71]

The same was true of the world of music, in which the emergence of early icons like Village People, Elton John and Freddie Mercury reflected the growing acceptance of diversity in modern life. The Center for Talent Innovation, a leading think tank on workplace issues based in New York, recently declared that 'the ubiquity of positive images of gay men and women has shifted public opinion such that for the first time in the US, a majority of Americans favour LGBT equality'.[72]

Ian McKellen, the British actor who portrayed Gandalf in *The Lord of the Rings* films, sees change unfolding in the world of movies. 'When I became Gandalf, I think I was the only gay member of the cast,' he said in an interview. 'Now there are two gay dwarfs. There's a gay elf. There are six openly gay actors ... Who's to say that Gandalf isn't gay anyway?'[73]

WORLDS APART

FOR THE MILLIONS of gay people living in countries that still regard homosexual acts as criminal, fear and persecution remain a reality of daily life. Seventy-seven countries still outlaw homosexual acts between consenting adults, putting gay men and women at risk of arrest and imprisonment, and in five of these countries they may face the death penalty.[74] In addition to limiting the personal freedom of gay people, these laws also foster an environment of intolerance and fear.

Since 2009, Ugandan politicians have sought to expand existing laws that criminalise homosexuality. Known locally as the 'Kill the Gays' bill, it pushes for the death penalty in cases of 'aggravated', that is repeated, instances of homosexual acts. It compels doctors, friends, relatives and neighbours to report 'offenders' within twenty-four hours of an incident or face three years' imprisonment. 'There is no longer a debate in Uganda as to whether homosexuality is right or not,' the bill's author David Bahati said in a 2012 documentary. 'It's not.'[75]

At times, Ugandan newspapers have published the names, addresses and photographs of gay men and women.[76] In October 2010, the now defunct Ugandan newspaper *Rolling Stone* ran one such article with the headline '100 PICTURES OF UGANDA'S TOP HOMOS LEAK'. A bright yellow banner said 'HANG THEM'. John Bosco, a former banker from Uganda, sought asylum in the UK after a radio station identified him as a homosexual in 2001. The UK government deported him in September 2008, just months after Britain's Home Secretary, Jacqui Smith, declared that gay men and lesbians could avoid harm in countries that criminalise homosexuality by being 'discreet'.[77] By the time Bosco landed in Kampala, newspapers had published his picture on the front page. He was arrested, thrown in a concrete jail cell and chained to several other prisoners. 'You are beaten by the police and then you are beaten by the inmates,' he says.[78] Bosco bribed his guards and went into hiding for six months while a legal team in the UK worked to challenge his deportation. He returned to the UK in March 2009 and now works as a mental health support worker and part-time bookkeeper in Southampton.

Ugandans tend to believe that homosexuality is 'un-African', and assume that gay men only have gay sex in exchange for money. A staggering 96 per cent of its population apparently believes that 'homosexuality should not be accepted by society.'[79] Advocates of the bill prey on those beliefs as a way to shore up their own power. They make gay men and women scapegoats in order to distract people from the problems that actually affect them, such as the economy and healthcare. Stirring anxiety about homosexuals gives the government some breathing room elsewhere.

Something similar may be taking place in Russia, where President Vladimir Putin appears to be behind a drive against homosexuals. It began in June 2013 with the passage of a homosexual 'propaganda' bill.[80] It imposes fines and jail terms on those who provide information to minors that may cause 'a distorted understanding' that gay and heterosexual relations are 'socially equivalent'.[81] The legislation is worded vaguely such that it could be used against teachers and parents who endorse tolerance towards gay people.[82] 'Pro-gay' foreigners and those suspected of being gay can also be arrested and detained for two weeks.[83] Following separate legislation, gay couples, and single parents living in any country that recognises same-sex marriage, can no longer adopt Russian-born children.[84]

At times, the Russian rhetoric has been reminiscent of that of the bureaucrats in Italy in the wake of the bubonic plague. Putin has justified his laws on the grounds that the Russian birth rate is falling and that the Russian family is in decline.[85]

Advocates of the bill have been less subtle. Dmitri Kisilev, the deputy director of Russian state television, has said that

Putin should go further. '[Homosexuals] should be banned from donating blood and sperm,' he said on Russia's most popular news programme. 'And their hearts, in case of an automobile accident, should be buried in the ground or burned as unsuitable for the continuation of life.'[86]

I met Putin frequently between 2000 and 2007. Our relationship was cordial, but we never strayed on to personal matters. As with other heads of state, I discussed the economy, oil and the balance of power in business partnerships with him. I have no sense of his attitudes towards sexuality, but I know that Putin is a pragmatist. To me, Russia's anti-gay legislation is more about political posturing than it is about a sincere disgust for gay people. As others have pointed out, it is likely that he is seeking to divert attention from other restrictive laws, passed at the end of 2011 in the aftermath of mass protests, that more broadly limit civil rights.[87] In an echo of persecutions of the past, the homosexual minority is being used as a pawn in the pursuit of power.

Regardless of the motivation, human rights organisations believe the laws will lead to an upsurge in anti-gay violence. In July 2013, the Spectrum Human Rights Alliance (SHRA), an advocacy group for gay rights in Eastern Europe, revealed how the followers of one neo-Nazi group had allegedly begun luring gay teenagers to apartments using same-sex personal advertisements. They then bullied and tortured them, before uploading videos of the ordeal to the Internet. 'Being outed in a small city or village in Russia very often means death,' Larry Poltavtsev of SHRA has said. 'Exposed teenagers may commit suicide, or they'll be harassed by their peers, their parents may kick them out of their house. It's a nightmare.'[88]

Progress remains uneven, but there is reason to believe that change will come more quickly than in centuries past. In an age of connectivity, glaring abuses of power are less likely to go unnoticed and more likely to draw a visible response. In August 2013, during the World Athletics Championships in Moscow, foreign athletes spoke out against Russia's anti-gay laws. Emma Green Tregaro, a Swedish high jumper, painted her nails in the colours of the rainbow in support of gay rights. American Nick Symmonds dedicated his 800 metres silver medal to gay and lesbian friends. Both drew international headlines. For the 2014 Winter Olympic Games in Sochi, Russia, the US sent a delegation with gay and lesbian sportspeople and President Obama declined to attend in any official capacity.[89]

Outside the arena of sport, world leaders from US President Barack Obama to UK Prime Minister David Cameron are increasingly connecting gay rights with human rights. In April 2013, UN Secretary-General Ban Ki-moon launched a global campaign to repeal anti-gay legislation around the world. Speaking in a video at the Oslo Human Rights Conference, he argued that culture, tradition and religion can never justify denying someone basic rights. 'My promise to the lesbian, gay, bisexual and transgender members of the human family is this: I am with you. I promise that as Secretary-General of the United Nations, I will denounce attacks against you, and I will keep pressing leaders for progress.'[90]

Laws like those in Russia should give us pause for concern. However, we must remember that all societies develop at a different pace. In recent decades, politicians in other countries have enacted similar legislation, only to repeal it years later, often with a profound sense of embarrassment and shame. Russia's recent legislation has a British precursor. In 1988, Margaret Thatcher's Conservative government passed a Local Government Act, Section 28 of which stated that local authorities 'shall not intentionally promote homosexuality or publish material with the intention of promoting homosexuality' and defined gay partnerships as 'pretended family relationships'. This stiffened the spine of both gay rights advocates and future politicians. Today the UK is one of the world's most tolerant societies for gay men and women.

Foreign governments can nudge leaders in Moscow and other capitals that repress gay men and women, but ultimately change must be driven from within. Jonathan Cooper, the chief executive of the London-based Human Dignity Trust, says that one country does not generally serve as a role model for another when it comes to LGBT legislation. For instance, the Bahamas de-criminalised homosexuality in 1991, but nine other Caribbean nations have kept anti-sodomy laws on the books. 'There is always this allegation that de-criminalisation is another form of neo-colonialism,' he says. 'This is, of course, absurd.'[91] In Commonwealth countries, once part of the British Empire, a colonial legacy is the criminalisation of homosexuality.

The homophobia that has shaped so much of gay history is diminishing, but the stories in this chapter serve as the backdrop to our thinking today. From ancient Greece to the Third Reich, and from the repression of Kampala to the freedom of New York, a long history of social liberalism mixed with destructive homophobia underscores every discussion and decision of today. We do not start with a blank slate.

CHAPTER THREE

DEEPLY HIDDEN

IN MAY 2007, the *Daily Mail*, a British tabloid, was aggressively leading the coverage of my sensational exposure. Its editors gave my resignation top billing, running more than twenty articles on the drama over the course of the month. I accept that changes in the leadership at Britain's biggest company were newsworthy and of public interest. I also know that details of my personal life were somewhat exaggerated and were used to sell newspapers. Some of the coverage seemed to celebrate my downfall, and much of it appeared homophobic. Astonishingly, six years later, in July 2013, a representative from the *Daily Mail* phoned my assistant asking if I would like to write an article arguing the case for gay marriage. I politely declined.

In spite of my history with the tabloid, I appreciated the offer. The newspaper's remarkable turnaround, from sending photographers to doorstep me to offering me a platform to speak on gay rights, reflects society's shifting attitudes towards gay men and women. This is demonstrated most starkly by the public's opinion on same-sex marriage. In 1983, half of those Britons surveyed said that same-sex relationships were 'always wrong'. By 2012, that figure had fallen to just 22 per cent.[1] Attitudes have even moved among religious groups. In 1983, almost 70 per cent of members of the Church of England strongly disapproved of same-sex relations. By 2010, that proportion had almost halved.[2] Among people with no religious affiliation, the percentage dropped from 58 per cent to 21 per cent over the same period.

The UK legalised same-sex civil unions in 2005 and, in 2013, proposals to legalise same-sex marriage easily passed through both houses of Parliament. In the House of Lords, the margin of victory was more than two to one.[3] Gay rights campaigners were not the only people pleased with the outcome. UK Prime Minister David Cameron, whose Conservative party was once referred to as 'the nasty party' for, among other things, passing anti-gay laws, was exuberant. 'I think we should think about it like this – that there will be young boys in schools today who are gay, who are worried about being bullied, who are worried about what society thinks of them, who can see that the highest Parliament in the land has said that their love is worth the same as anybody else's love and that we believe in equality,' he said. 'I think they will stand that bit taller today and I'm proud of the fact that that has happened.'[4]

The winds of change are sweeping through the US as well. According to the 2007 Pew Global Attitudes Survey, 49 per cent of the US agreed with the statement: 'Homosexuality is a way of life that should be accepted by society'. By 2013, 60 per cent of Americans did.[5] In the first three months of 2013, seven national polls on same-sex marriage in the US all reached the same conclusion: that support for gay marriage had now exceeded opposition to it.[6]

Opinion polls are not the only barometer of progress. President Obama repealed the US military's 'Don't Ask, Don't Tell' policy in 2011. One year after that, a study co-authored by academics from all four US military academies found that ending the ban had no negative consequences on 'military readiness or its component dimensions, including cohesion, recruitment, retention, assaults, harassment or morale'.[7] Successful television shows from *Glee* to *Downton Abbey* feature gay characters. And even Pope Francis has called for the inclusion of gays in society, saying he has no right to judge them.

Such broad cultural shifts have given businesses the opportunity to embrace change in this area. More than 90 per cent of Fortune 500 companies have policies that are designed to prevent discrimination, including on the grounds of sexual orientation.[8] Blue-chip companies from aerospace to banking to big oil now proclaim their achievements.

In spite of that progress, it is estimated that 41 per cent of LGBT employees in the US remain in the closet at work, as do 34 per cent of their counterparts in the UK.[9] The reasons employees hide their sexual orientation are deeply personal and extremely complex, and they vary from person to person. But it is clear that fear of damaging their career progression underlies that decision.

These closeted employees certainly lack role models: at the end of 2013, there was no openly gay CEO in the Fortune 500. I do not think that this is due to a dearth of talent among gay executives. Rather, the lack of representation in the upper echelons of business seems to stem from issues of self-selection and inclusion. Anxiety still grips LGBT employees, from the factory floor all the way to the chief executive's office.

Brian McNaught, who *The New York Times* once dubbed the 'godfather of gay diversity and sensitivity training'[10], conducts seminars in the workplace and has worked with corporate giants including AT&T, Goldman Sachs and Merck. I agree with his view that closeted employees have a tendency to think that a catastrophe will accompany their coming out, regardless of their sector or the protections in place at their company. As he says, 'Those who don't come out have generally created dramas in their heads of what might happen but rarely, if ever, does.'[11]

The fear that closeted employees experience made it difficult to secure some of the interviews for this book. My colleagues and friends asked their closeted friends and family members to participate. Many declined, even when offered the protection of anonymity.

A heterosexual woman who works for an Atlanta-based company describes the difficulty of asking her closeted friend, who is in his mid-twenties, if he would consider an interview. He is extremely sensitive about the topic. 'I couldn't even send him an email or leave him a voicemail describing why I wanted to talk to him,' she says. 'I had to leave a voicemail asking him to just call me back. And even when he did call me, he had to call me later when he could find an empty office and not be in his open-air cubicle.'[12]

Others agreed to interviews, only to cancel them at the last minute without any explanation or follow-up. Closeted employees who did agree to speak requested that their real names not be used. Some asked that details such as age, nationality and even the city where they work be removed to obscure their identity further. Most stressed that they should not be contacted via their work email. As one of them wrote, 'This is my personal email address. Please use this one for correspondence on this issue from now on. Prevents the PA asking difficult questions.'[13]

The paranoia is present even among employees who work at firms known for embracing LGBT inclusion. George, an investment banker, is a case in point. Educated at Oxford University, he has spent the past six years working at the London office of one of the US's largest banks. His employer is regarded as having one of the most gay-friendly workplaces, as judged by surveys in both the US and the UK. He has never experienced homophobia in the workplace. His company sponsors a number of charities that advance gay rights. And, in his words, the firm has 'gone hell for leather to create massive diversity programs that promote inclusion'.[14] This includes bringing in openly gay athletes to speak about their experiences and creating a programme in which straight employees place posters and stickers on their office doors to indicate a safe space for their gay colleagues.

Yet among the 300 people who work on George's floor, no one is openly gay. 'I think the real problem with banking is there are no senior people who are out,' he says. 'I know there are four or five of us on my floor, but none of us are open about it.'

He and his closeted workmates believe that coming out opens them up to professional risk. Stickers cannot change that. Surveys may demonstrate that more than 70 per cent of people in the UK support gay marriage, but a significant minority do not.[15] That, he says, is something he has to consider, particularly when it comes to his performance appraisal.

Every year, employees must submit a list of people who are able to assess their performance. At the same time, managers seek unsolicited comment from employees who are not named on the list, which is common practice at large banks. The results of these reviews determine how much employees are paid, whether they will be promoted and essentially their long-term viability in the firm.

'While you think there is a 99-per-cent chance coming out will be fine, the consequences of that 1 per cent are terrifying,' he says. 'If someone doesn't like me, he doesn't need to be in my face about it or rude or homophobic. He can be very smart and just say in my review that I didn't handle clients very well. He can just make up a story and all of a sudden my ranking is in jeopardy.'

There are safeguards around the procedure: the human resources department does its due diligence and teams are consulted on discrepancies in performance. But that does not comfort George, whose elaborate analysis explains away even those safety checks. 'Once a bad review drops, your team is spending time and money trying to defend your ranking rather than trying to promote you. They have to play defence rather than offence. And this could all be from one comment.'

Making those kinds of calculations on a daily basis is exhausting, especially when the working day sometimes stretches to sixteen hours. So too is having to obscure details of what you did over the weekend, changing the pronoun used to refer to the person you are dating and making sure you do not accidentally reveal aspects of your life on social media. Even giving an interview for this book meant avoiding coffee shops near his office and visiting one ten minutes away. George was open and attentive throughout the interview, but discussing these matters in public gave him some cause for concern. As he sipped his coffee, he seemed to monitor fellow customers and passers-by. Occasionally he whispered his answers.

George is not alone in having to adjust the truth and alter basic aspects of his daily routine. According to the Center for Talent Innovation in Washington DC, 18 per cent of gay men modify some aspect of their lifestyle, such as where they socialise after work, so that they can 'pass' as straight; 16 per cent admit to changing their mannerisms and voice; while 12 per cent of lesbians say they adjust aspects of their appearance, such as their clothing, hairstyle or accessories.[16]

'I am tired of having to lie to people,' George says. 'Given the job I do and the hours I work, it affects quite a large chunk of my life. It is critical that I am happy and honest in that part of my life going forward.' He says he will come out once he becomes a director or managing director in a few years' time. For now he will just have to keep up his cover.

George's employer has made a highly praised push for inclusion. Yet the personal assessment of the risks, and a degree of paranoia, still prevent some employees from bringing their true selves to work. For gay men who work in more hostile workplaces, the situation is even tougher. Alexander, not his real name, says homophobic banter from colleagues pushed him deep into the closet during his nine-year stint as an investment banker in New York City and London. He is no longer closeted, but does not want to reveal his identity for two reasons. First, he does not want to identify and shame colleagues who treated him poorly. Second, he believes that tacit homophobia still exists in the workplace, even if most of his colleagues are accepting of gay people. 'I am still a member of the financial community and intend to have business interests in my city for a long time to come,' he says. 'Members of the financial community would doubtlessly look unfavourably on me breaking the "code of silence".'[17]

'It's not the type of thing where you can say I was overtly threatened or called a faggot,' he says during an interview in the privacy of his apartment. 'But it's clear tacit homophobia exists. It makes you wonder if you're allowed to be yourself when you're at the office.'[18]

Most of the comments he heard came from a managing director who was also his line manager. One week the team travelled from London to a stately home in the Welsh countryside for an off-site meeting, a company tradition designed to build camaraderie through biking, hiking and canoeing. One night over dinner the group of mostly male bankers went around the table and each person revealed one thing someone had whispered to them in bed. 'I said, "Someone told me that I've got very nice arms,"' he remembers. His boss, who was sitting at the other end of the table, yelled back at him, '"Well, what was *his* name?"' Alexander had no choice but to laugh along with everyone else.

The jibes continued the following day when the team headed to a bike trail. 'As we were walking to the bikes he said, "Do you see that pink one? That one is for you."'

He also recalls driving from a meeting in Switzerland with a well-regarded female managing director. They were discussing another managing director who had recently left the firm. She started making disparaging comments about his decision to return to university and his close relationship with his mother. 'She said very derisively, "He probably came out too." I said, "Well good, I hope he's happy." She turned and stared at me with her mouth slightly agape.'

Although the firm has an LGBT group, Alexander says the stigma attached to joining means 'it was only for assistants and HR'. No bankers actually attended its meetings. He did have one confidant: another closeted banker from the firm who he bumped into once at a gay nightclub. He advised Alexander to remain closeted and to hide every sign. 'He said, "You will never find proof of it, but there's a glass ceiling. You can progress to managing director, but no further. If you're gay you are not part of the club."' Alexander eventually came out, and was let go from the firm six months later. He tries not to think about whether homophobia played a part, and likes to believe that his redundancy had more to do with the recession than some form of discrimination. Now out and working as a strategy consultant, he is pleased to have left his old colleagues behind. Working in a new gay-friendly atmosphere has helped him see just how stressful his old life was.

'In the closet, you always need to ask yourself how you are behaving and if people will perceive something that you don't want them to perceive,' he says. 'It's like being on stage, but, in your head, it's not a matter of whether or not the audience likes you. It's a matter of whether or not you have a job.'

The fact that George and Alexander would only be interviewed on the condition of anonymity shows that hidden fears still exist. Erika Karp, the founder and CEO of Cornerstone Capital, Inc., understands their anxiety. Karp says it is only on the outside of the closet that one can truly understand the toll that hiding takes on a person inside.

She spent seven years in the closet while working at Credit Suisse in New York. She felt intense pressure to keep her sexuality a secret. 'There's a male energy on Wall Street and you have to be perceived as being absolutely on top of your game,' she says. 'You want to be evaluated and judged based on your contribution. When you're lesbian, it adds a level of difference that people might be uncomfortable with, or at least distracted by. That takes away attention from what your mandate is.'[19]

In spite of being in a long-term relationship with a woman named Sari, she spoke to colleagues about her partner Sam. She got very good at switching 'she' to 'he' the moment she stepped into the office. The constant lying created a barrier between Karp and some of her closest colleagues, and drained her of energy. Inevitably, the stress of keeping up appearances bled into her personal life. 'I remember when Sari and I were walking in Central Park. I don't have all that good vision. I would think that 100 yards off I was seeing someone from my office. I would get stressed out and drop Sari's hand. That was so painful.'

Karp lived her life openly among friends and family. She viewed her first gay pride parade as a moment of celebration, until the route approached her office block. 'I left at 30th Street, walked way far west and down ten blocks,' she recalls. 'The idea of walking past my office was painful. I remember the feeling of stress and fear.'

The threat of homophobic rejection is not the only reason some women stay in the closet. Gay and bisexual women also say that some men are fascinated by their sexual orientation. That can put them into awkward situations and create a major barrier to business performance.

Chloe is a confident, outspoken twenty-eight-year-old who works as a team leader in the oil and gas division of a major international services firm. She knows several openly gay employees and describes her colleagues as open-minded. She doubts that anyone would regard her sexual orientation as wrong. Yet she asked that I not reveal what city she works in. 'I have proven myself,' she says in the basement of a dimly lit bar, 'but I'm scared that men are going to take me less seriously.'[20]

Experiences that she had outside her current job have shaped her view on the matter. A trained geophysicist, she started her career at one of the world's largest oil and gas groups. She worked alongside rig crews drilling oil wells; she was always the only woman on site. Every night, her colleagues would down at least six beers each and engage in sexual banter.

Once, during a long break between assignments, her team was sitting in a meadow. Someone had arranged for food to be delivered, along with a pair of strippers. 'There were two naked women on drugs, and they were dancing in front of twenty men and touching each other,' she says. 'Most of those people were roughnecks. They were saying disrespectful things about women, and they only had positive thoughts about women when there was a sexual connotation.'

Worried about spurring them on, Chloe never thought about coming out. Eventually, her unhappiness led her to swap the oil rigs for a place in graduate school. She hoped to live her life, authentic to her true self, in the open with everyone and not just with close friends. She casually revealed to her class-mates that she was bisexual. Within days, one of them, who had spent years working at an investment bank, propositioned her for sex. 'He said, "You are clearly open to many things sexually, so let's do this." He loved the fact that I am bisexual,' she says.

She declined and their relationship soured. But her class-mate continued to proposition her and discussed her situation with other students. 'The level of harassment was intolera-ble,' she says. 'I didn't have enough strength to manage it.' Chloe promptly returned to the closet and refused to discuss her private life.

Her current employer actively fosters an inclusive envi-ronment. However, Chloe remains in the closet. 'You cannot succeed if you're gay,' she says. 'The oil and gas industry is so old-fashioned that nobody in their right mind would come out.' She remembers my own resignation well. Her hetero-sexual colleagues said that I should have been more open and transparent, but Chloe strongly believes that I did the right thing by denying who I was. 'If you're at the heart of this industry, it's a huge risk,' she says. 'I was on the rigs. I know exactly what the industry is like.'

My resignation reinforced her belief that she has to stay in the closet. This is the wrong lesson to draw from my experi-ences. The double life I led should not be seen as a workable blueprint for a business career. It should be viewed as a cau-tionary tale.

THE COSTS OF HIDING

AS ALL THESE employees know too well, a decision to conduct your life in the closet is not a neutral one. It involves strad-dling two worlds. You will be sapped of mental energy as you switch from one to the other, even if you are well prac-tised. This energy could be used far more productively, whether in business to solve problems, or in private life to build a stable relationship with a partner.

Sexuality does not exclusively define anyone, but it is undoubtedly a significant portion of their identity. Denying a part of yourself makes it impossible to accept all of yourself. This takes an enormous toll on confidence and self-esteem. As I found, you may not even be able to recognise that cost. Dr Jack Drescher, a psychoanalyst in New York, says people in the closet cannot always appreciate their personal and pro-fessional achievements. 'They feel they're being false and don't know who they are, so they cannot fully take in their actual accomplishments,' he says. 'This is the psychology of the closet. In the process of throwing up a smoke screen so that others can't see you, you also can't see things going on around you. You can't see yourself.'[21]

As I progressed in BP, I made my calculations and consid-ered the trade-offs that would be necessary. I reached the top, though when I got there I felt trapped and isolated.

My double life began in Anchorage, Alaska, in 1969. I spent my first weeks in a dump of a hotel with walls so thin that you could not help but get to know the other guests. The city was recovering from an earthquake, which had destroyed much of the downtown area. You could still see that a large amount of the city centre had just sunk away. There was a street of bars where people would get beaten up and occasionally shot. Even so, they would go there nightly to drink. At one of the bars of choice, the management covered the floor in peanut shells so that you would make a crunching sound with every step. People danced on pianos.

Amid all this commotion, I started my first job, assisting with the flow testing of exploration wells. The men with whom I worked were big and burly and came from Texas and Oklahoma. They could have passed for escaped convicts. In the many hours we spent in the frozen north waiting for the next thing to do, I began to develop a method of hiding my personality. It was a matter of behaving completely normally and not rocking the boat. I was polite and helpful. I was twenty-one but looked all of seventeen. I was not only the youngest person on the team but also a foreigner, so people generally wanted to support me. Whenever anyone asked if I had a girlfriend, I would say 'yes' and that was that. People were reserved at the workplace. That created a barrier behind which I hid.

The standards of business conduct in the late 1960s and early 1970s were much lower than those of today. So too were ideas of what was appropriate to make people feel included and part of a team. On trips to Los Angeles and San Francisco, we would work all day. At night, the entire group would head to a strip club to drink whiskey or gin and to chain-smoke. Women, dimly lit by flashing lights, would wiggle around. It was appalling and I was not fond of going, but I never refused. I had to blend in.

In 1971, after my two-year stint on the tundra, BP finally transferred me to New York. I found some relatively cheap accommodation near the corner of 48th Street and Second Avenue, in a place that is now called Dag Hammarskjold Plaza. It was a one-room efficiency with a minute kitchen and next to no charm.

I did not know how to handle myself in such a big and bustling city. But the anonymity it afforded gave me the courage to venture out to a gay bar for the first time. The bouncer stopped me at the door. 'This is a gay bar,' he said, as if to warn me off the place. 'You know this is a gay bar, right?' I was so embarrassed that I rushed away. Maybe I did not look the part. I had been wearing a suit, so I came back a few hours later dressed in jeans and a sweater.

I was on edge when I finally went in. I had expectations that I would see something exciting and out of the ordinary. However, the normality of the scene shocked me; it was merely a large number of people drinking and dancing. And some of them were in suits.

I did not have much money in those days, and so I was not a frequent visitor. Gay clubs were widely regarded as places for sex. But I discovered that people's actual motivations for going were less clear. I was meeting a cross section of people, some of whom were interesting, and many of whom could only live their gay life within the four walls of a club.

At that time, BP had a rather small office in New York. That helped put me at ease. I could not imagine that anyone else in the office would be gay, let alone going out to a gay bar. I was wrong. Within weeks, as I walked into one of these bars, I was immediately spotted by someone who looked familiar. It turned out that he was someone from the office. He came up to me and I wanted to sink through the floor.

He was significantly more engaged with the gay scene than I was. Because of that and his position within the company, I assumed he had much more to lose if his sexuality were revealed. As with my early encounters as a teenager, I understood that he was also at risk and that he would not let on to anyone where he had seen me. At work, our mutual secret terrified me, but nobody noticed and we never tripped up.

In letters home to my parents in the UK, I would carefully edit my life. I would have been open with them about my move to Greenwich Village with a Frenchman, who had a girlfriend and taught me how to cook and throw dinner parties. I would have been more reticent about my fascination with David Hockney, the outspoken, openly gay artist who treated homosexuality directly in his paintings. At some point, I purchased his erotic illustrations of poems by Cavafy, which featured men in bed together. Looking back, perhaps it was veiled rebellion. I would not have been open with them about my secret gay life.

Whether writing to my parents or attending meetings, my underlying philosophy was 'give no evidence, make no sign, give no excuse for people to see the real you'. Any perceived slip-up could put me on edge for weeks. Once, when I was walking past a construction site in a light blue suit, a group of builders started catcalling and chanting gay slurs. I vowed to wear only dark suits from that day forward.

In 1974, I arrived in San Francisco and worked there for two years. I returned in 1980 to complete a business degree at Stanford. The city did not suit me. For a reserved Englishman who had not come out, the thrusting atmosphere of the Castro District simply did not appeal.

Throughout this time I had a girlfriend, the daughter of my doctor. I would see her at weekends and would much look forward to spending time with her. She was a good companion. I still made a rare appearance in the Castro gay bars, but the gay scene in San Francisco was so segregated from the rest of the city that I saw little risk in being outed, as I knew I would not bump into her. If you live two lives, you can rationalise everything.

At least one person knew that I was not what I seemed. All business-school students had pigeonholes for their mail. One day, my pigeonhole contained an invitation to attend a gay and lesbian meeting. I thought about it, but in the end I did not go. A few days later, the student who had organised it came up to me and said, 'I'm sorry you weren't there.' Perhaps he understood the struggles that lay ahead for me. My girlfriend eventually ended our relationship. I could not blame her. I had no intention of getting married and she sensed that. I went on to roles in Calgary, London and Aberdeen. By 1986, I had risen to the post of chief financial officer of the Standard Oil Company in Cleveland, Ohio. I had largely stopped meeting my gay friends. My mother had moved in for good.

I was approaching forty and everyone wanted to pair me off with their friend or cousin. I would go to a dinner party and someone's spouse would say, 'I've got a really nice person I'd like you to meet.' It was getting to the stage of my being probably one of the most eligible bachelors for a divorced woman with a couple of children. I would be polite, but show little interest. If I gently ignored the questions, they tended to go away.

PROFESSIONAL HIDING

IN 2013, I was having lunch with the Russian ambassador to the UK at his residence. My long-standing business acquaintance, Russia's former energy minister Yuri Shafranik, was the guest of honour. The ambassador recounted in vivid detail how, in 1989, I had met Shafranik when I was leading BP's exploration and production division. 'We treated you very well at the time because our intelligence showed that you were going to be the next CEO of BP,' he said. 'Our agents picked that up.' I wondered what else was in their files.

During the fourteen years my mother lived with me, I largely severed myself from any form of gay life. I felt a deep sense of loneliness, but thought I could get by with a very rare one-night stand. My paranoia went up in 1995 after I became chief executive. When I was travelling abroad, I was often a government guest and there were security people around. After BP acquired Amoco in 1998, my profile grew in the US, so I also had personal security there around the clock. Security personnel would stay in rooms adjacent to mine, and the moment the door opened they would be woken up. The closet door was now nailed shut.

My fear of being discovered arose from my belief that I could not do business as an openly gay person in a country that criminalised homosexuality. That was true in places as far apart as the Middle East, Angola and Nigeria. I viewed being in the closet as a practical business decision.

It does not take the Russian intelligence service for some-body somewhere to know when an employee is in the closet. I managed my public identity extremely well, but in hind-sight I know some colleagues suspected that I was gay. I was good at deluding others, and even better at deluding myself in the process.

In June 2002, I delivered a speech at the Women in Leadership conference in Berlin. My argument was straight-forward. BP would remain committed to diversity in order to attract a disproportionate share of the most talented people in the world. It was only by seeking out the best and bright-est people from all walks of life that we had a chance of maintaining a competitive edge. 'That is the simple strategic logic behind our commitment to diversity and to the inclu-sion of individuals: men and women regardless of background, religion, ethnic origin, nationality or sexual orientation,' I said. 'We want to employ the best people, everywhere, on the single criterion of merit.'

Our approach to inclusion cut across all diverse groups. But when the left-leaning *Guardian* newspaper reported on the story the next day, their headline emphasised a narrow slice: 'Diversity drive at BP targets gay staff'.[22]

The emphasis on sexual orientation demonstrated how

unusual it was to mix 'gay' with 'business'. At BP, we did just that and included same-sex partner benefits in the menu of things we should rightly provide to our employees.[23] In late 1999, the world's largest public oil company Exxon merged with its smaller rival Mobil. Prior to the merger, Mobil had extended benefits to same-sex partners, but Exxon did not. As part of the merger, Exxon refused these benefits to new recruits.

The headline in *The Guardian* came as a bit of a shock. But more worrying were the interviews that directly probed my personal life. As chief executive, every interview was a potential minefield. A sloppy turn of phrase or misplaced sentence could spell disaster.

With regards to my sexual orientation, I learned to dissemble without flinching. I did not need to practise the lines. I did my best to give the impression that I was a bachelor who had not met the right woman. 'Whether I get married remains to be seen,' I once told *The Sunday Times* of London, and I added, 'Maybe this interview is an advertisement.'[24] The *Financial Times* was the only newspaper to ask directly whether I was gay. A straightforward question received a straightforward reply: 'You have got the wrong man there.'[25]

The most worrying interview, however, occurred in 2006. Producers at the BBC had asked me to appear on *Desert Island Discs*, a popular radio programme in which one 'castaway' chooses eight records they would take with them to a desert island. Pieces of music are interspersed with a largely biographical interview.

Why worry? Because in 1996, the show's host Sue Lawley asked Gordon Brown, then the Shadow Chancellor of the Exchequer, about his sexuality. 'People want to know whether you're gay or whether there's some flaw in your personality that you haven't made a relationship?' she asked in a matter-of-fact way. Brown replied, 'It just hasn't happened.'[26]

Roddy Kennedy, the head of press at BP, was a very shrewd man. I am fairly certain he had seen through my veil, but he did not want any speculation about my sexual orientation to interfere with BP's image. From his point of view, that was a correct position to take. He approached me with his concerns, and I think he used his considerable influence to make sure the host did not probe my sexuality. He managed it and the question never came up.

Just for a moment I had wondered whether to use the programme to come out. Had I said, 'I want to do it,' Roddy would have managed it. But my courage was short-lived and I kept that thought to myself.

Instead, I talked about Giacomo Puccini and Richard Strauss. I reminisced about the freezing cold of my boarding school and recounted my mother's harrowing personal history. It was all very friendly. When she asked me what luxury item I would take to the island, I said a box of Cuban cigars. I would smoke them while listening to Francisco Repilado's 'Chan Chan' and watching the sunset.

Reality was a far cry from that imaginary idyll. I was getting increasingly weary of running two lives. It makes no difference what you are doing; if you are doing something in secret, it wears you down.

Even today, I hear so many stories of young people hiding in the closet. That makes me both angry because of the pressure that society is putting on them, and sad because of the consequences. The stories in this chapter bring back memories of encasing myself in a hard shell and making sure that no one got inside it. People might speculate. They might ask questions. But I was convinced that no one should get close enough to see the real truth, or the real me.

Regardless of their level within a company, employees cannot have perspective when they are trapped in the closet. It is only in hindsight that they can understand the limits created by a double life and of its corrosive effect on work and life.

Alexander, the former investment banker, still remembers his boss's taunt about riding a pink bicycle. But rather than getting angry at his old colleague, he gets angry at himself for staying in the closet for so long. 'If I had just been honest with everyone from the start, would my life really have been so difficult?' he asks. 'Homophobic people hold the power because we allow them to hold it. If we allow them to make us feel shame, we will remain second-class citizens.'

Fear kept him in the closet. Now freedom keeps him out.

'What's the fun of telling me there's a pink bike if I'm proud of being gay? It's only funny because I'm trying to stay in the closet. Coming out kills the joke.'

CHAPTER FOUR

PHANTOMS AND FEARS

IS THE FEAR of coming out justified? In what context should a decision like this be considered? And what impact does it have? In my own case, I was terrified about coming out. In retrospect, that fear was not entirely justified. As my career progressed, so did society's attitude towards gay employees. Anxiety and panic prevented me from seeing that progress clearly.

I have never experienced any explicit negative consequences of coming out, so I have asked others to tell their own stories in this chapter. There is a reasonable body of evidence that indicates that, at the highest levels in companies, LGBT people are statistically under-represented. In addition, there is significant bias, both conscious and unconscious, against LGBT workers. This results in many practical inequalities, from unequal pay and benefits to overt discrimination. Six people who have come out tell their stories of how their managers made their sexual identity a barrier to their progress. And one business owner tells his story of the financial consequences on his business and of the harassment he experienced as a result of being gay.

The lesson of history and that of today is that minorities are used as scapegoats when things go badly for society. The history of the Jews, for example, is well known. LGBT people are also a minority and it is still uncertain whether the improving attitude towards inclusion is permanent or simply part of a cycle that could reverse.

During his tenure as a top executive at the Ford Motor Company, Allan Gilmour had to make calculations on a daily basis. Not all of them involved numbers. In the late 1980s, a journalist asked Gilmour why he had never married. 'I told him that I was married to the Ford Motor Company,' Gilmour says. Unaware of any other gay executives at the Dearborn, Michigan, headquarters, he felt the need to dissemble and deflect conversation from his sexual orientation. 'I did not think that I would be fired if I were out or outed,' he says. 'But I thought it could be detrimental to further progress in the company, and that it could attract unwanted attention to Ford.'[1]

Gilmour rose to become vice chairman, the second most senior position in the corporation, spending thirty-four years in the closet in the process. Whispers about his sexuality followed his ascent. In the early 1990s, a reporter approached the public relations office while investigating a transgression made by another Ford executive. 'The PR person allegedly said, "Forget about that. I'll give you a real story. Gilmour is gay."' Another employee in the public relations office later confirmed what had happened.

Nothing came of the incident, and later that year, Red Poling, Ford's CEO at the time, told Gilmour that he was on track to succeed him. However, the board ultimately appointed Alex Trotman to the role. Gilmour decided to retire.

Gilmour says he does not know whether his sexuality played a role in being passed over, though others have suggested that it did. In 2002, when Ford re-hired Gilmour as its vice chairman, he met with chief executive Bill Ford, who had recently discussed Gilmour's appointment with the board. 'He said to me, "You being gay never came up,"' Gilmour remembers. 'I could be wrong, but I translated it to mean, "Isn't that interesting, because it has come up in the past."'

As much as society's attitudes are changing, and as much as corporations are embracing that change, coming out will always present risks. Gilmour's story illustrates that the consequences of coming out, and of being outed, will never be completely clear. The hidden nature of prejudice means that there are risks about which an employee could be totally ignorant.

These risks vary by industry, employer and region. In the US, it was only in late 2013 that the Senate passed a bill explicitly protecting LGBT employees from workplace discrimination. That bill still faces a tough fight in the House of Representatives.[2] Only twenty-one states have passed laws explicitly protecting LGBT employees. In the outdated legal environment of the twenty-nine other states, it is theoretically possible for an employee to be fired for being gay.

In the US, almost two in every five gay and lesbian employees who are out report that they have been harassed in their workplace in the last five years.[3] Among white-collar lesbian, gay and bisexual workers, more than half say they have been snubbed or slighted, including by 'off-colour jokes and subtle jabs'.[4] When I was establishing my career, those figures would have been considerably higher.

Since I was outed in 2007, I do not think that my sexual orientation has reduced my prospects. But I speak from an atypical position. I came out after I had had a successful executive career and after I had made contacts across industries from oil and gas to finance over four decades. Before I came out, I made it to the top of BP without the stigma of being perceived as an outsider. A young person who comes out at the start of his or her career might be denied the opportunities that I was given.

Years of progress have reduced the risk of harassment, but they have not completely eradicated it. I cannot say with any

certainty that someone's career will be unaffected if they disclose their sexual orientation. I wish I could tell gay people
that they will be fine, but the evidence collected here suggests that there remain some risks. On average, these are small
and diminishing, but as this chapter demonstrates, individual
circumstances vary significantly.

AT THE TOPS OF CORPORATIONS

CORPORATIONS ARE THE engines of human progress. They
are designed to bring us health, wealth and happiness, which
no single individual could attain on his or her own. But when
it comes to diversity and inclusion, corporations tend to be
followers rather than leaders, reacting rather than being pro-
active. In response to changes in society, corporations have
set up mentoring programmes, adjusted their corporate policies, invested in diversity training and boosted recruitment
activities that target under-represented groups. But in spite of
that effort, the representation of minorities in corporate life
remains disproportionately low.

That bias begins in the boardroom, which is dominated by
straight, or at least apparently straight, white men. In 2012,
white men held almost three-quarters of all boardroom seats
at Fortune 500 companies.[5] Data suggest that they are becoming more entrenched as the average age of independent
directors increases.[6]

Surveys of the diversity of boardroom members have so
far not measured the presence of LGBT people. So we do
not know how many are on boards. In 2013, Sally Susman,
a communications executive at Pfizer who is openly lesbian,
was appointed a non-executive director of WPP, the multinational advertising and public relations firm. Her view is

that it will take some time before boards will become representative of gay people. 'It has traditionally been an inside
game that's disadvantaged women, minorities and gay
people,' she says. 'Change will be slow, but it is coming.
The real heroes here are the CEOs and nominating committee chairs who look to an individual's talents and beyond
their labels.'[7]

Among headhunters, there is debate about whether the
situation is actually improving. Anna Mann, a headhunter of
choice for board appointments to many FTSE 100 companies, says that sexual orientation is not a consideration during
the selection process. 'I have never come across any form of
prejudice against gay people at board level,' she says. 'It is an
irrelevant factor.'[8] However, another distinguished City
headhunter, who wishes to remain anonymous, sees plenty
of scope for prejudice. 'The point of recruiting people to
boards is people want kindred spirits,' she says. 'That may
well exclude people who are not identical to people who are
recruiting them.'[9]

This is not proof of discrimination; the reality is much
more complex. Corporate boards are the product of established social and professional networks, and are tasked with
the stewardship of a company. It is therefore unsurprising
that they tend to be conservative and risk averse, and that
they have behaved in ways that reinforce the division between
insiders and outsiders. For example, I have seen male directors attempt to close deals or to argue a point while standing
at the urinal, thereby excluding female members of the board.
I believe that for executives making high-level decisions,
homosexuality might raise a conscious or unconscious red
flag, since someone who does not fit the board's mould brings
with them risk and uncertainty. This may explain why, at the
end of 2013, there was no openly gay chief executive among

FTSE 100 corporations. One board has appointed an openly gay chief executive[10], who is expected to take up the position at Burberry in the summer of 2014. If we were to assume that 5 per cent of the population is gay, there should be five gay chief executives among FTSE 100 companies, and some twenty-five in the Fortune 500.

HIDDEN BIASES

WE ARE ALL guided by unconscious biases that shape our behaviour. From an early age, we take in information and absorb negative stereotypes from society, our friends and our families, and this information shapes our beliefs and attitudes towards other people. Psychologists Mahzarin Banaji and Anthony Greenwald detail the phenomenon of unconscious bias at length in their book *Blindspot: Hidden Biases of Good People*. 'These bits of knowledge are stored in our brains because we encounter them so frequently in our cultural environments,' they write. 'Once lodged in our minds, hidden biases can influence our behavior toward members of particular social groups, but we remain oblivious to their influence.'[11]

The Implicit Association Test (IAT) demonstrates that all sections of society are subject to hidden biases.[12] The test asks participants to associate groups of people (such as Hispanic people, old people and gay people) with evaluations (such as good and bad) and stereotypes (such as intelligent, athletic and evil). The faster the participants can sort and pair groups with evaluations and stereotypes, the stronger is the association. Research consistently indicates that people more easily associate the concept of good with white, young or straight people than they do with black, old or gay people.[13]

By the end of 2013, more than one million people had completed the IAT that measures biases related to sexual orientation. 'The vast majority of heterosexual people who take the test show some level of implicit preference for straight people,' says Rachel Riskind, the psychologist who oversees the data. 'Lesbian and gay people demonstrate a very slight preference for other gay or lesbian people, but it is not nearly as strong as the pro-straight preference among straight people.'[14] Recently, I decided to take the same test. My own results placed me in the 16 per cent of participants who display an automatic preference for gay people over straight people; 68 per cent of test-takers preferred straight people over gay people and 16 per cent showed no preference.

We are exposed to society's heterosexual bias from an early age. The vast majority of characters encountered by children in books and on TV are straight; in religious settings, homosexuality is frequently associated with sin; gay men in the US are not allowed to donate blood because of lingering fears about AIDS; and, depending on the jurisdiction, some rights afforded to heterosexual people, such as the right to marry and adopt children, are not afforded to gay men and women.

Stereotyping gay people as flighty, promiscuous, infected with disease and prone to drug and alcohol addiction inevitably colours judgements of their abilities. When assessing a series of job candidates, a manager has only so much time and so many resources with which to evaluate them. If there are any gaps in his assessment, however, his brain fills them in, partly guided by unconscious biases and stereotypes. It is an automatic process, critical to the successful evolution of the human race, but one that can damage the chances of minorities in the modern workplace.

Research on gender and race already demonstrates that unconscious biases may affect decisions relating to hiring, promotion and pay, and a growing body of evidence suggests the same may hold for gay job applicants. Sociologist András Tilcsik tested the hypothesis that gay men are significantly less likely to secure job interviews than heterosexual men with identical qualifications.[15] He identified almost 1,800 advertisements for job vacancies in seven states and submitted two fake résumés for each position. Within each pair of résumés, one applicant listed experience in a gay student organisation at university. The other applicant listed experience as the treasurer of a small left-wing campus organisation called the 'Progressive and Socialist Alliance'. The résumés were designed to be sufficiently distinct but not to project any relationship between qualification and sexual orientation. Any difference in the rate at which applicants were invited for an interview could therefore only be attributed to the 'gay signal' coming from one student's experience.[16]

Of the applicants designed to be heterosexual, 11.5 per cent were invited to an interview. From the pool of equally qualified applicants who had worked for a gay organisation, only 7.2 per cent were invited to interviews. That means that gay applicants were around 40 per cent less likely to be interviewed.[17]

That result is not simply attributable to an explicit aversion to hiring gay men. Stereotypes, both conscious and unconscious, may have played a role in selection. As Tilcsik explains, gay applicants in the study received fewer invitations to be interviewed than usual when they responded to job advertisements that explicitly sought candidates who were 'assertive', 'aggressive' and 'decisive', three stereotypical traits of heterosexual men. A manager rejecting a gay applicant may not be explicitly homophobic. Yet his or her unconscious assumptions, including the belief that gay men are feminine and passive, could make the gay applicant seem unfit for the job.[18]

When openly gay men do secure a job, they may be more likely to earn lower wages than their straight male colleagues. A dozen studies published in the US in the past ten years have found that gay men earn between 10 and 32 per cent less than their heterosexual male colleagues with similar characteristics.[19] A review of research conducted in Australia, Canada and Europe found that gay men earned between 7 and 15 per cent less. In most cases, there was no discrimination against lesbians.[20]

Economists argue that this disparity might be more than a penalty against gay men. It might also reflect a premium for married men, who consistently earn more than single heterosexual men.[21] In an effort to explain that apparent premium, some have suggested that more productive men get married,[22] while others have suggested that marriage makes men more productive[23] and that employers therefore favour married men.[24] The wage premium for getting married is also likely to be at least partly a result of a preference for heterosexual workers.[25] Whatever its origin, the premium is real and it is used as a tool for advancement. Straight men frequently note in their professional biographies that they are married and have children.

Addressing these disparities will not be easy. 'There is a very strong stereotype that gay people are affluent and well-educated,' says economist Lee Badgett. 'That might push back against any thought or fear that management is treating people differently in the workplace.'[26] Because companies are only now beginning to track the sexual orientation of their employees, few are able to identify potential discrepancies in pay.

Lesbians, however, tend to earn more than their heterosexual female colleagues. There are several possible explanations. Because lesbian women are less likely to have children, they do not experience delays in their career progression as frequently as heterosexual women.[27] Research has also shown that, compared to straight women, they work longer hours and, on average, have obtained higher educational qualifications.[28] That behaviour may be part of a strategy for survival, in which lesbians realise that they will not marry a man who will be likely to command a higher salary, and therefore overcompensate in the pursuit of economic security. The earnings advantage may also be a reward for perceived masculinity.[29] In any case, earning more than straight women does not put lesbians on an equal level with men. Women, gay or straight, earn less than both gay and straight men.[30]

EXPLICIT BIASES

THE CONSEQUENCES OF being gay in the workplace could be more than just financial. A homophobic manager can create great discomfort for all the gay employees below him. This affects motivation, morale and the likelihood that a gay person will thrive professionally.

Hillary, a consultant at a major international consulting firm in London, was too nervous to come out when she joined her firm as a junior employee in 2012. She worried that she would be known as 'the lesbian' as opposed to a young woman who was good at her job. On one occasion, she accidentally used the pronoun 'she' in front of a more senior male colleague when referring to her partner.

'I explained that I was a lesbian and had a girlfriend and it all seemed to be fine, but I was in the office the next day and the manager was telling everyone on the team I had a muscular boyfriend called Dwayne,' Hillary says. 'I thought it would be a one-off joke, but needless to say the jokes continued and it became quite unbearable. I asked him to stop but he didn't. My humiliation seemed to give him satisfaction, especially when others on the project asked me how Dwayne was.'[31]

This went on for months until the seemingly homophobic manager left the project. It was only then that Hillary felt comfortable enough to come out. 'The majority of people do not see sexuality as an identifier,' she says. 'However, as with everything, there is always the exception to the rule.' Despite being out, Hilary still chose to remain anonymous in this book because she did not want people to think the firm was homophobic. She is not remaining anonymous because she thinks her sexual orientation would reflect poorly on the firm.

A manager has the power to set the tone for the entire team. When leaders think it is funny to make homophobic jokes, the group will tend to laugh and mimic their behaviour. This leaves gay employees feeling marginalised and powerless to speak up. That was very much the experience of Aidan Denis Gilligan, who worked as a project manager at a leading international public relations firm in Brussels. On several occasions, a senior manager sent sexually aggressive emails from a gay colleague's computer to junior employees and blind copied other members of staff who were in on the joke. 'A young junior trainee on a six-month trial would think that the gay guy was hitting on him, which would lead to a panic,' Gilligan says.[32] At a company Christmas party, the homophobic manager gave an employee a gift, which he had to open in front of the entire staff. It contained a latex glove and a jar of Vaseline. Whenever Gilligan walked past the manager's office to use the toilet, the manager would ask, 'Are you going to the "laddies" room?'

Gilligan says that homophobic jokes and slurs discouraged gay employees from attending social events at work, which further alienated them from the leadership. The final straw came at his second company Christmas party. A British man seated at Gilligan's table was wearing a kilt. When the head of the office stopped by the table, she asked the man if Gilligan had been feeling him under the table. 'It was professionally humiliating to the extreme. She was giving licence to everyone in the company to make fun of me,' he says. 'It was clear I'd never get to the top of the tree there because I'd never fit into their model.'

Margaret Regan runs a global organisation that has led training courses in diversity and inclusion for some of the world's largest companies and organisations. She says the overwhelming trend points towards inclusion, with more and more companies seeking to foster supportive environments for their LGBT staff. Things have come a long way. In the 1990s, a senior manager at a client company once asked her not to bring gay consultants to their offices for the organisation assessment they were conducting. When she refused, they asked that she encourage them to stay in their hotel rooms in the evening. She cannot imagine receiving a request like this today.

Religion can play a role in the anti-gay attitudes that are manifest in some workplaces. In 2011, Regan worked with a client who had difficulty discussing LGBT issues. 'The second in command lectured us about what the Bible says about gay people,' she says. 'We looked at each other and didn't know what to say. She told us that, "You have to hate the sin, but love the sinner."'[33] Regan's team also asked managers to assess how various groups felt about the office environment. 'We had a question about how gay and lesbian staff feel working there,' she says. 'One executive said, "I will not answer. I don't discuss that."'

Regan believes that the regional differences in the US are still there, and that some executives are still not ready to make LGBT issues part of their overall diversity and inclusion strategy. However, as society's viewpoint changes, so will the views of many of these executives. They are now the outliers rather than the norm.[34]

Coming out can drive a wedge between gay employees and their religious managers. Justin Donahue spent eight years working for one of the world's largest aerospace companies. While working in the Florida office, he invited his female manager to attend a concert put on by his gay choral group. She was visibly uncomfortable during the concert. During their performance of 'Kiss the Girl' from The Little Mermaid, the choir had a lesbian couple kiss each other on the lips. His manager got up and walked out. The following Monday she called Donahue into her office. 'She was visibly shaken and really uncomfortable. It was obvious she was on the verge of tears, and really offended,' he says.[35] She raised her voice throughout the conversation, telling Donahue that she was praying for him and that she wanted to call his mother to let her know that he was a good employee in spite of leading a gay lifestyle. 'I just sat there and tried not to get upset,' he says. The events of that day put a strain on their relationship. Donahue eventually transferred to another office in California.

Anti-gay attitudes are not the only risk that gay employees face when they come out. Popular culture frequently depicts gay men as frivolous and irresponsible. There is a risk that managers, even open-minded ones, will take them less seriously. It is not an overtly hostile attitude. It can, however, affect whether managers give gay employees the same levels of respect as their straight counterparts.

Jacob spent more than five years working as a writer at a major media company in London. He says that his sexuality frequently coloured his managers' view of him. Once, when he was describing a story on the persecution of minorities, a manager responded, 'Oh, that sounds fabulous!' while making her wrist go limp. Another time, a very senior male manager said that Jacob should not 'waste himself on quirkiness' and that his stories were 'too light'. Jacob was confused, as he had recently reported stories about riots, prostitution and drugs. 'They have a preconceived notion that gay people are fluffy and look for evidence, perhaps unknowingly, to confirm their bias,' he says. 'How can you advance when people aren't judging you by your actual work?'[36]

He left the company in 2012. His former colleagues later told him that his editor had mocked his sexual orientation during a meeting. 'She was explaining Twitter etiquette and told them they were representing the company and should watch what they say. She claimed that she had repeatedly told me "not to Tweet about gay clubbing". I've never done that. If I were heterosexual, I doubt she would have used a clubbing example. But gay people are often the butt of the joke, even among relatively liberal people.' Jacob is another example of someone with deep-rooted fears who, despite being openly gay, wished to remain anonymous in this book in order not to jeopardise his career prospects. 'Managers generally don't care if you're gay,' he says. 'But if you voice concerns about mistreatment, you're suddenly seen as a liability.'

Transgender employees appear to face the most severe consequences for coming out. In one US survey, 90 per cent reported experience of harassment and discrimination on the job, while nearly half believed they had been fired, not hired or denied a promotion because of their identity.[37] The unemployment rate for transgender people in that sample was more than twice the national rate. In 2007, Vandy Beth Glenn was working as an editor and proofreader of legislative bills at the

Georgia General Assembly in Atlanta. In September of that
year, she revealed that she would be transitioning from male to
female the following month. Sewell Brumby, the chief legal
counsel for the Assembly, summoned Glenn to a meeting to
confirm her intentions. 'As soon as that meeting was over, I
was marched back to my desk, given a couple of boxes to pack
up my belongings and hustled out the door,' she says.[38]

Glenn sued for unfair dismissal on the grounds of sex discrimination. In court depositions, Brumby did not question
Glenn's performance. Instead, he said that 'Glenn's intended
gender transition was inappropriate, that it would be disruptive, that some people would view it as a moral issue and
that it would make Glenn's co-workers uncomfortable'.
He also argued that 'it's unsettling to think of someone
dressed in women's clothing with male sexual organs inside
that clothing'.[31]

It was not until 2011, four years after Glenn was dismissed,
that she won the right to return to work. She did not receive
any back pay. 'A lot of people don't see the purpose of trans
people in the LGBT movement, but I think it's as simple as
this,' Glenn says. 'We're all hated by the same people for the
same reasons. We violate gender norms.'

Not even self-employed gay people are immune to prejudice. Bob Page, a businessman in North Carolina, has grown
Replacements Ltd. into the world's largest retailer of china,
crystal, silverware and collectibles, with annual revenues of
more than $80 million. Page came out in a news article in
1990, and has had to contend with intermittent attacks on his
business ever since. Churches have asked their congregations
and other churches to avoid doing business with Replacements.
Vandals have sprayed gay epithets in the store's bathrooms and
on its outdoor facilities. Several years ago, a woman parked her
car across the two-lane street leading to Replacements. She

shouted about 'the coming of the Lord' and the evils of homo-sexuality. Police removed her forty-five minutes later. 'I've been very visible,' Page says. 'We're not naive enough to think that there aren't people out there who hate our guts and mine specifically.'[40]

Opposition swelled in the run-up to North Carolina's referendum to ban gay marriage in May 2012. In the preceding months, Page lobbied legislators and rented two double-sided electronic billboards in support of gay marriage. The company received numerous emails, letters and telephone calls from angry customers. 'I will not do business with a company that openly supports sexual perversion,' a customer from nearby Raleigh wrote in an email. 'Please take me off your mailing list.' Another customer suggested Page's activities threatened the happiness of his children. 'I have a wife of 26 years and four daughters,' the letter said. 'I am very concerned that with an increase in visibility and acceptance of the gay and lesbian lifestyle, one of my children, who would have grown up and been happily married to a husband, could be tempted to the lesbian lifestyle.'[41]

Page has lost local business for being out and for publicly supporting gay marriage. However, since the advent of the Internet, business in his store has become less important; only 5 per cent of his sales are derived from it. He is also free of the chains that limit corporate leaders. 'One letter said I was doing a disservice to our stockholders,' he says. 'The reality is I am the stockholder. I only have to answer to myself.'

LESS AND LESS FEAR

WITH THE PASSAGE of legislation and, most importantly, of time, gay employees have fewer and fewer reasons to fear direct discrimination and its consequences. The stories of homophobia in the workplace that I now encounter, including many of those in this chapter, are increasingly stories of individual prejudice rather than a discriminatory corporate culture. Consistent and institutional harassment is giving way to isolated incidents of inappropriate behaviour, which are often more of an embarrassment for the perpetrator than for the target. But coming out can still complicate the professional lives of LGBT employees: it requires them to admit that they have misled their colleagues and that they have not been themselves. I have been asked whether coming out could give colleagues a reason not to trust someone, and the answer undoubtedly depends on the context. Someone who grew up in the homophobic environment of my childhood might be forgiven for coming out later in life. Today, as society changes, I am not so sure.

The benefits of coming out in business – and in particular, of coming out early – are beginning to outweigh the risks. This does not mean that homophobic views and heterosexual bias have disappeared. In some instances, homophobia even appears to be on the rise. In the US, for example, the number of reported hate crimes against gay people has actually increased since the mid-1990s.[42] In France, fewer people now think that homosexuality should be accepted as a way of life than in 2007.[43] After the French Parliament legalised gay marriage in 2013, reports of hate crimes against gay men spiked dramatically.[44] The lack of LGBT representation in senior corporate positions suggests there are factors that still limit career progression for LGBT employees.

I have seen first-hand how the remarkable legal and social changes that have taken place around the world in recent years have contributed to a more tolerant corporate environment. But as this chapter makes clear, there is still a long way to go. We must not assume that the wave of positive change will continue indefinitely. History suggests that successful and prosperous societies are more accepting of minorities, but that minorities are used as scapegoats when societies experience difficulty. Defending and advancing the rights of any minority takes constant vigilance, because societies do not always learn from historical calamity. Jonathan Sacks, the former Chief Rabbi in the UK, has described his own fears of a reawakening of widespread anti-Semitic feeling. 'I used to think that the Holocaust had cured us of this idea; that it was impossible not to hear from the ghosts of Auschwitz the cry, "Never again." Now I am not so sure. I have come increasingly to the view that if we do not, like Jacob, wrestle with the dark angel of our nature and beliefs, there will be other tragedies.'[45]

Today the number of anti-Semitic incidents around the world is increasing dramatically.[46] There may be no connection between these trends and homophobia. It is, however, sobering to see that countries from the US to France to Russia have seen an upsurge in homophobic violence.

At the end of 2013, there were an astonishing seventy-seven countries in which homosexual acts were deemed a criminal offence. They serve as a stark reminder of how far many countries have come, of how far we still have to go and of how far we could fall back unless we continue to improve inclusion. Provided we do this, and I believe we are doing so, the risks to coming out are becoming smaller and smaller. One of the most important catalysts for change is the growing recognition that coming out is good for business, the subject of the next chapter.

CHAPTER FIVE

COMING OUT IS GOOD BUSINESS

ON 2 JUNE 2013, I wrote an editorial in the *Financial Times* arguing the case for gay marriage. The House of Lords would vote on a measure legalising same-sex marriage the following day. I supported the bill as a pragmatic legislator, as a gay man and as a human being. But I also supported it because I am a businessman.[1]

Business does not usually take a position on the institution of marriage. But, in my time as chief executive, I learned that any policy that fosters an inclusive environment makes good business sense. Paul Reed, my former colleague at BP and now a senior executive there, puts it best: 'I don't want people saving a quarter of their brain to hide who they are. I want them to apply their whole brain to their job.'[2]

Inclusion creates a level playing field, which allows the best talent to rise to the top. Respecting diversity of sexual orientation and gender identity should therefore be recognised as a matter of strategic importance to every company competing in the global market for talent. Minorities who are not treated fairly and who do not feel included will choose to work elsewhere. More and more companies now understand that. As a result, they are providing greater support for the rights of LGBT employees.

In November 2008, voters in California had the option to vote on Proposition 8, which would overturn the right of two people of the same sex to get married in the state. Ahead of the vote, only four big businesses and organisations publicly expressed their support for same-sex marriage.[3] By March 2013, when the United States Supreme Court heard cases on the Defense of Marriage Act (DOMA) and Proposition 8, a total of 278 employers, including more than 200 companies, had given their support to 'equal marriage' in an amicus brief filed with the Court.[4]

In that brief, companies including Apple, Citigroup, Microsoft, Morgan Stanley and Starbucks argued that 'far from creating uniformity, DOMA obliges employers to treat an employee married to someone of the same sex and an employee married to someone of a different sex unequally', noting that business outcomes depend 'on the talent, morale and motivation of the workforce'.[5]

The behaviour of companies today suggests that the risk of losing the support of those opposed to LGBT equality is now outweighed by the benefits of inclusion. In January 2012, Starbucks announced that its support of same-sex marriage 'is core to who we are and what we value as a company'.[6] By March, the National Organization for Marriage (NOM), earlier formed specifically to support Proposition 8, had launched its 'Dump Starbucks' campaign, which called on members to boycott the coffee giant. The company had, it said, 'declared a culture war on all people of faith' and that its customers were funding a 'corporate assault on marriage'.[7] Within a week, 10,000 people had joined NOM's Facebook page, and more than 23,000 had signed its online petition.[8] One year later, at the Starbucks' annual shareholders meeting in Seattle, an angry shareholder stood up to complain. He suggested that the company's support for same-sex marriage had contributed to 'disappointing' earnings in the first full quarter after the boycott. Starbucks' chairman and chief executive Howard Schultz replied that 'not every decision is an economic decision ... We employ over 200,000 people in this company and we want to embrace diversity. Of all kinds.' As the audience cheered, he left the offending shareholder with some parting words. 'If you feel, respectfully, that you can get a higher return than the 38 per cent you got last year, it's a free country. You can sell your shares.'[9]

Leaders on Wall Street have also been outspoken. In 2012, Lloyd Blankfein, the chairman and CEO of Goldman Sachs, appeared in a video supporting same-sex marriage. The video was produced by the Human Rights Campaign, the largest LGBT advocacy group in the US. Blankfein asked viewers to 'join me and a majority of Americans who support marriage equality'. He later admitted that because of that statement the firm had lost at least one major client, whose leadership objected to his stance on religious grounds.[10]

He continued to articulate his business logic in a round of media appearances, implying that the loss of a client matters less than the ability to recruit the best minds. 'I'm trying to have a neutral workplace environment that is as inviting as it can be for all people,' he told CBS News. 'To the extent there are other companies or industries which are going to be hostile and repellent to people who are talented ... they're just giving us a comparative advantage.'[11]

Diversity and inclusion are not the same thing. Having a certain number of employees from diverse backgrounds will do little to help a business unless those employees are made to feel welcome and valued. Inclusion is undoubtedly more difficult when it comes to LGBT people. A company can tell if its employees and applicants are male or female, or Asian or Hispanic. But it is not always clear who is a member of the LGBT population and who is not. It is therefore crucial that a company's support for equality and inclusion is unambiguous.

In the US, around 80 per cent of LGBT respondents to one survey said that when applying for a job it was 'very important' or 'fairly important' for their potential employer to have an LGBT equality and diversity policy already in place. In the UK, 72 per cent of respondents agreed.[12]

Julia Hoggett, a managing director at the London office of Bank of America Merrill Lynch, remembers how important the right tone of acceptance was to her in the mid- to late 1990s, before she had come out. Presented with job offers at two separate banks, she compared salaries, training programmes and locations. She also assessed whether being open with her sexual orientation would put her at risk. 'In one particular clause of the contract, one firm effectively said "we will not sack you on the grounds of sexuality" and the other firm remained mute,' she remembers. 'The other firm only said what it had to under the law, which was that you could not discriminate on the grounds of gender and race. I chose to work for the firm that protected LGBT employment rights because I felt that it would be a more embracing place, in part since they had gone through the thought process to include protections for lesbian, gay and transgender employees in the UK when the law did not require them to do so.'[13]

The war for talent is the principal reason that an increasing number of Fortune 500 companies see LGBT inclusiveness not as an option but as a necessity. In 2002, 61 per cent of those companies included sexual orientation in their corporate policies. Only 3 per cent included gender identity.[14] By 2014, 91 per cent prohibited discrimination on the basis of sexual orientation and 61 per cent protected employees from discrimination based on gender identity.[15] There was also a dramatic jump in the number extending company healthcare benefits to same-sex partners. That figure grew from 34 per cent to 67 per cent over the same period.[16]

Policies are an important place to set the right tone. Their application is measurable and is capable of being tracked, and that provides a concrete benchmark for assessing a company's commitment to its gay employees. Good companies can transcend the variety of legal frameworks in which they operate, and can make their policies work even where legislation does not require them to take action. That is essential for any business that wants to attract high achievers from all backgrounds.

The Human Rights Campaign understood that when it launched its Corporate Equality Index (CEI) in 2002. It laid out its expectations of how US companies should treat their LGBT employees and LGBT consumers. It then evaluated employers annually against these expectations.[17]

In the first year of the CEI, only 4 per cent of the companies they examined obtained perfect scores.[18] Those companies included Intel, JPMorgan Chase and Xerox. By 2011, 55 per cent, or 337 in total, had adjusted their policies and benefits systems to obtain a perfect score.[19] The list of those companies receiving the highest marks included firms from traditionally conservative sectors; among them was the mining and metals giant Alcoa, and oil and gas firms BP, Chevron and Shell. By contrast, in 2012, oil and gas giant Exxon became the first company ever to achieve a negative score, a position it maintained for the following two years.[20]

Competitive rankings like the CEI help provide important incentives for change. In 2005, the defence contractor Raytheon became the first company in its sector to obtain a perfect CEI score.[21] The company was widely praised for its achievement, especially as it operates in a sector dominated by a male, blue-collar workforce, traditionally not a comfortable environment for LGBT employees. One year later, three of Raytheon's competitors, Boeing, Honeywell International and Northrop Grumman, introduced changes to help them achieve the same success.[22]

The CEI criteria have become more demanding over time to keep up with society's growing expectations for the treatment of LGBT people. Companies are therefore forced to keep improving their policies to stay competitive. That is encouraging, as inclusion requires constant reinforcement and vigilance.

Changes at several companies have been remarkable. The conservative city of Louisville, Kentucky, is not the first place you would think of when discussing LGBT inclusion. Nor is Brown-Forman, the beverage business that owns labels including Jack Daniel's and Finlandia vodka. But when it received a score of just twenty on the 2009 CEI, its leaders took notice. The company's newly appointed chief diversity officer, Ralph de Chabert, worked through each of their policies to improve their score, seeking advice from his counterparts who had overseen changes at other companies.

He dispelled the myth that providing same-sex partner benefits or covering the cost of gender reassignment surgery would be as expensive as some people feared. At the end of the day, with so many other companies making changes, it became an issue of 'Why aren't we?'

The company became the first in Kentucky to achieve a perfect CEI score. More important are the changes de Chabert sees on the ground. Gay employees now bring their partners to work events, and some have told him they feel more accepted at the company than they do in their own families. This is also reflected in the fact that the company's LGBT employee group has more members who are heterosexual supporters than members who identify themselves as LGBT. Heterosexual employees have come to understand that they need their gay colleagues as much as their gay colleagues need them.

'It's far more costly for people to be in the closet, it's just that you don't see the impact,' de Chabert says. 'The impact is that you don't get the creativity, productivity and innovation that you would have gotten otherwise.'[23]

HIDDEN COSTS

IT IS VIRTUALLY impossible to quantify the loss of productivity in percentages, or the loss of creativity in terms of dollars and cents. There is, however, robust evidence to suggest that companies pay a heavy price when employees do not feel comfortable enough to come out in the workplace.[24]

During the early 1970s, Louise Young taught at an Oklahoma college. In 1975, officials decided not to renew her contract after they learned that she had visited a lesbian bar. That experience turned her into an activist. She soon accepted a job as a software engineer at Texas Instruments. In 1993, she founded the company's LGBT resource group, and by 1996, she had convinced management to introduce a non-discrimination policy that included sexual orientation. But the following year the company sold its aerospace and defence arm, in which she worked, to Raytheon, which did not have a similar policy. Once again, Young found herself in a workplace without basic protection.

In 2001, Young presented on behalf of the LGBT resource group at a company diversity conference. She decided to speak about productivity. With the president of every Raytheon business on the front row of the auditorium, she had just three minutes to speak. She described a productivity index she had created that assumed a 10-per-cent productivity loss suffered by closeted employees who were trying to hide their sexual orientation. 'I want you to go back to your offices after this conference and shut the door. Then I want you to remove all vestiges of your family, particularly your spouse. Put the pictures in the drawer and take off your wedding band. You cannot talk about your family and where you went on vacation. And if your spouse or partner is seriously ill, you are afraid to acknowledge your relationships because you are afraid you might lose your job. Do all that and see how productive you are.'[25] Raytheon subsequently implemented a non-discrimination policy that covered sexual orientation and gender identity and expression, and extended domestic partner benefits as well as equity in all areas of benefits for its LGBT employees.

Closeted employees still grapple with those fears. However, corporations have done much to reduce the resultant stress. Today The Clorox Company is regarded as one of the most LGBT-friendly companies in the US, and it has obtained a perfect score on the Corporate Equality Index every year since 2006. The company has come a long way since Tom Johnson, now the company's chief accounting officer, began working there in 1988. At the time, sexual orientation was not included in the company's non-discrimination policy. There was no company network for LGBT staff, and the company did not extend domestic partner benefits to same-sex couples. Early on in his career with the company, Johnson could not identify one single openly gay senior executive. He had gone through therapy to come to terms with his own sexual orientation, but he simply could not bring himself to share his personal life with colleagues. 'The leaders at Clorox at that time were more conservative,' he recalls. 'There were no indicators that coming out would be in any way good for my career.'[26]

As he rose to become the vice-president of finance, Johnson spent the following nine years in the closet. During that time he remembers feeling trapped within himself. Like so many other closeted employees, he lied about his weekends and the fact that he had a long-term partner. He avoided asking personal questions of others because they would naturally ask similar ones. He particularly dreaded corporate presentations, which left him feeling exposed and self-conscious about his mannerisms and gestures. 'I wasn't sure what I might project to people, so I just stuck to the script, and I was dead on stage,' he says. 'I was responsible for mergers and acquisitions, and I wanted to convey my enthusiasm, but I couldn't. That impacted on my ability to be authentic.'

Clorox is a multi-billion-dollar consumer goods company. Employees are encouraged to draw on their personal experiences to think of new products to take to market. Johnson felt as though he was wearing a straitjacket. 'I was always putting my ideas through a filter and wondering, "Will it help them realise I'm not like them?"' he says. It consumed a lot of his energy and resulted in good ideas being suppressed.

Stories like Johnson's have encouraged the corporate world to regard the adoption of gay-friendly policies as directly contributing to profitability.[27] When companies put such policies in place, they also encourage employees to reveal their sexual orientation. According to the Center for Talent Innovation, two-thirds of LGBT employees are out at companies that provide health insurance benefits for same-sex partners compared to just half at companies that do not.[28] When asked in a 2009 survey why they were not open to everyone at work, nearly a fifth of closeted employees specifically cited a lack of policies to protect them, and a similar proportion cited a fear of being dismissed on the basis of their sexual orientation or gender identity.[29]

The survey also suggested that coming out reduces psychological stress and improves employee well-being. For example, 44 per cent of LGBT employees in the closet reported feeling depressed in the previous twelve months compared with just a quarter of those who are open to everyone at work.[30] It is therefore unsurprising that closeted employees are less satisfied with their jobs. Of closeted gay men, only 34 per cent reported that they were satisfied with their rate of promotion, while 61 per cent of those who were out reported that they were satisfied.[31]

Peter Sands, the chief executive of the multinational bank Standard Chartered, sums it up fittingly. He explains that being trapped in the closet is 'miserable for individuals and bad for business. In a world where business success is all about unleashing people's creative energy and imagination, it makes no sense to cripple so much talent.'[32] The evidence points in one direction: people are more satisfied and more productive when they can bring their whole selves to work.

Coming out does not just benefit the individual; it may also boost the productivity of that person's co-workers. Johnson says that being closeted created a barrier between him and the teams he led at Clorox. 'I felt like I was holding something back and others sensed it as well,' he says of the difficulty he had letting people see his real self at the time. 'The evasiveness and inability to be authentic created a level of distrust that undermined my ability to lead.'

This anecdotal evidence is supported by the results of controlled experiments. Psychologists at the University of California, Los Angeles found evidence to support their hypothesis that participants paired with an openly gay partner would outperform participants paired with someone ambiguously gay when given the same task.[33] They concluded that 'not knowing the identity of one's interaction partner may be more harmful to performance than knowing the identity – even a stigmatised identity'.[34]

Policies that support LGBT equality send broader signals about a company's attitude to its people. Claudia Brind-Woody, the co-chair of IBM's Executive Task Force for LGBT Diversity, tells a story she heard from one of her recruiters. He was representing the firm at an MBA career fair that targeted LGBT students from several prominent business schools. Throughout the day, a number of Asian women stopped by to pick up pamphlets from the company. Noticing their disproportionately high presence, he stopped to ask one of them to explain. 'All of you can't be lesbians, what's going on?' he asked. The woman confirmed his suspicion. 'No, I'm not a lesbian. But LGBT is the toughest category for you to crack. If you value and include LGBT employees, then I know you will include Asians and women.'[35]

Claudia's story is reinforced by other evidence that shows that a majority of heterosexual professionals have come to view the treatment of LGBT employees as a way of evaluating a potential workplace.[36] It is seen as an indicator of how seriously companies value diversity, tolerance and creativity.[37]

Like companies, cities are likely to thrive when the atmosphere embraces gay men and women. Sociologist Richard Florida has argued that there is an economic cost to intolerance that manifests itself in a city's ability to attract the so-called 'creative class'.[38] Economic success depends on openness to new ideas and people. Talented workers, the ones most likely to innovate, are drawn to areas known for diverse thinking and openness. Florida found that the single best predictor of an area's success in high technology was the scale of its gay population, even more so than the concentration of foreign-born residents.[39] The five US metropolitan areas with the highest concentration of gay couples were all among the most successful areas.[40] He also observed that areas experiencing little to no growth (Buffalo and Louisville, for instance) had low concentrations of same-sex couples. 'To put it bluntly, a place where it's OK for men to walk down the street holding hands will probably also be a place where Indian engineers, tattooed software geeks and foreign-born entrepreneurs feel at home,' Florida later wrote. 'When people from varied backgrounds, places and attitudes can collide, economic home runs are likely.'[41]

Many economists have also examined tolerance of homosexuality and its correlation with economic performance in the rest of the world. Marcus Noland, executive vice president and director of studies at the Peterson Institute for International Economics, found that attitudes towards gay men and women correlated highly with a country's ability to attract foreign investment and the level of its sovereign bond ratings.[42] He suggested that attitudes towards homosexuality may be 'part of a broader package of social attitudes towards difference and change, especially change that comes from non-traditional sources'.[43] Foreign investors may also link intolerant attitudes to 'unhelpful official behaviour and, in the extreme, attacks on foreign-affiliated facilities or staff'. Elsewhere, political scientist Ronald Inglehart has argued that the acceptance of gays and lesbians is the most sensitive indicator of an advanced society's well-being because homosexuals are typically 'the least-liked group in most societies'.[44] Essentially, he called them the final frontier of diversity.

HIDDEN STIGMAS

AT BP, I used to think that by being in the closet I was training myself for very complex problem solving. I could keep so many balls in the air simultaneously and make sure they did not collide. I had two lives that were self-contained, and on the few occasions they came into contact, I did my best to get each back on track. In order to do that, I had to filter everything I said to remain consistent and pay close attention to how others perceived me.

Anyone who has grown up harbouring a potentially threatening secret develops similar skills. Psychologists have suggested that people living with concealable stigmas, including gay people, rape survivors, people with eating disorders and poor people, must carefully monitor their social environments and learn to manipulate their public image in response to constantly changing and unpredictable social situations.[45] This suggests that there is a strong chance that gay people who enter business bring a unique set of skills that they can leverage for a company's benefit and their own advancement.

As Kirk Snyder points out in his book *The G Quotient*, the experience of growing up as outsiders may foster other skills, including adaptability, creativity and intuition.[46] Psychologists have noted that, when embracing their own sexual orientation in the face of society's expectations, members of the gay community develop a heightened sense of perception. This experience forces them to think deeply about their feelings from an early age, and to consider constantly the reactions of others, from their parents to siblings to strangers, each of whom could potentially reject them. Navigating those situations and pondering the outcomes leads to a high degree of self-awareness.[47]

At the same time, they have become adept at reading people and situations. This ability to process information may be an adaptive mechanism to cope with the climate, or *perceived* climate, of anti-gay violence.[48] Being able to pinpoint threats becomes a matter of survival. At the same time, the ability to size people up may arise partly from the prolonged search for potential romantic partners: it is not always obvious who is gay and who is not.

Gay people hone their sensitivity to situations by having come through adversity. This might explain why gay managers are apparently better at motivating their employees. In his study of more than three thousand employees over five years, Snyder found that employees working for gay male managers demonstrated significantly higher satisfaction with their jobs compared to the typical US employee. He was struck by how, at a time when job satisfaction was declining across the US, employees led by gay managers appeared to be thriving. Subsequent investigations and interviews revealed that these employees were not responding to their managers' sexual orientation but to a certain style of leadership.[49]

'Because of the experience that gay people have had, they're much more likely to value that single mother, the person of colour, and diversity in all its forms,' he says. 'In our study they proved to be much more motivational and more focused on the employee as an individual.'[50]

MARKETS

IN 2008, THE Campbell Soup Company hoped to target the LGBT population by placing an advertisement in the *Advocate*, the highest-circulation gay magazine in the US. First printed in December of that year, the advertisement featured a lesbian couple and their son preparing dinner with Swanson Chicken Broth, one of Campbell's products. The right-wing American Family Association, an organisation that promotes fundamentalist Christian values, objected strongly. The group contacted its list of more than three million email subscribers to ask them to write to Campbell's CEO to express their outrage.

'Campbell Soup Company has openly begun helping homo-sexual activists push their agenda,' the message read. 'Not only did the ads cost Campbell's a chunk of money, but they also sent a message that homosexual parents constitute a family and are worthy of support. They also gave their approval to the entire homosexual agenda.'[51]

Its activists began to bombard the company's website with negative comments. They said they were no longer going to buy Campbell's soup and that they would be returning their existing purchases to their local shops. Douglas Conant, the company's CEO at the time, sought the view of Rosalyn Taylor O'Neale, his chief diversity officer. She recalls giving him two pieces of advice.

'The first,' she remembers, 'was "Know that this too shall pass. It's a two to four week issue and at the end of that they will go on to annoy someone else. Ride it out."' Her second point emphasised the business case for placing the advertise-ment in the first place. 'We advertise in the *Advocate* because we sell soup to gay people and we want LGBT people to buy soup and crackers and all of our other products. Explain to them that we advertise in Hispanic and Latino publica-tions, in African American publications and women's publications. It's about advertising in publications where our consumers are.'[52] The company stood by its action, thou-sands of consumers wrote in to thank them and the protest eventually stopped.

A marketing strategy aimed at a diverse population is essential for any business: in order to grow it needs to reach as many new consumers as it can. The LGBT population, traditionally under-served by marketers, presents a meaning-ful and often sizeable opportunity. Discretionary spending by gay men and lesbians is growing. The overall buying power of the LGBT market in the US is estimated to have reached roughly $830 billion in 2013[53], up from $743 billion in 2010.[54] In the UK, it is estimated that the gay market is worth at least £70 billion.[55] Allan Gilmour, the former chief financial officer at Ford Motor Company, has famously described his company's marketing push to gay people in these terms: 'I know a lot of lesbians and gay men buy automobiles. I just want my unfair share.'[56]

So does everyone else. Companies observe that 58 per cent of LGBT adults say they are more likely to purchase everyday household products and services from companies that market directly to them.[57] In recent years, that marketing has moved from gay-only publications to mainstream magazines, and from gay-only television networks to mainstream channels.

In 2012, the retail giant JCPenney hired Ellen DeGeneres as its national spokesperson. During an investor presentation, the CEO framed the move as part of broader changes to keep the company, which was founded in 1902, relevant to young people. 'We're fine with growing old,' he said. 'We're not fine with growing stale.' It later released a Father's Day advertisement showing two gay men playing with their children.

MillerCoors, the second-largest brewer in the US, has published a series of print and digital advertisements for Coors Light beer that featured young couples of the same sex dancing and touching each other, underneath the heading 'Out is Refreshing'. And clothing chain Gap has run billboards featuring two men sharing one T-shirt with the tagline 'Be One'.

Bob Witeck, the president and founder of Witeck Communications, based in Washington DC, has worked in LGBT marketing for more than two decades. He has helped devise strategies to market to gay households for firms including American Airlines and Marriott International, among other corporations. He says that advertisements appealing to the gay consumer send a signal to the broader market that a company is contemporary, forward-thinking and relevant. That is crucial for businesses that hope to capture the attention of young consumers. Even in the most conservative circles, young people are more accepting of LGBT people than their parents. 'They want to know gay people,' he says of today's teenagers and twenty-somethings. 'LGBT marketing isn't just to influence the 5 to 8 per cent, but the 50 to 75 per cent who want to see the world they live in welcome their gay teacher or best friend or cousin.'[58]

Buying a billboard and plastering it with images of apparently gay men will not make a lasting impact. The gay consumer is increasingly wary of gimmicks, and instead seeks a sustained, sincere commitment to LGBT issues. That is one reason why the Human Rights Campaign launched its popular 'Buying for Workplace Equality Guide' in 2006. It uses CEI scores to divide businesses into three categories. The categorisation aims to affect the way people make purchasing decisions, and millions of consumers have consulted the guide. 'We get letters all the time from people letting us know how they use the Buyer's Guide to make their own purchasing decisions,' says Deena Fidas, the director of the Human Rights Campaign's Workplace Equality Program. 'For example, "My partner and I were deciding between a Toyota and some other brand, and we went with Toyota because of their high score in the Buyer's Guide."'[59]

Bill Moran is the head of Merrill Lynch's National LGBT Financial Services Team, which exists to meet different retirement and tax planning needs of gay people. 'It's a big opportunity,' he says. 'When you look at all the niche markets that are out there, this is the only one that has special legal and tax considerations that the other markets don't have.'[60]

Heterosexual advisors routinely approach Moran to learn how they can move into the space. 'They'll say, "Can I as a straight guy penetrate this community?"' he says. 'My response is, "Yes, if you care." If you're just in the space because you recognise the wealth that's there, you're not going to be successful.'

As this chapter demonstrates, businesses are increasingly concerned with LGBT inclusion. There are many senior executives within the boardroom who understand and respect the need to attract and support LGBT employees. However, it is naive to assume that businesses are always sincere or driven purely by goodwill. Corporations do not work that way and we should not ascribe human characteristics to them. Rather, we should focus on the factors that motivate change.

Legislative progress, such as the decision to strike down the Defense of Marriage Act in the US, will nourish momentum. So too will generational change as individual leaders and employees share their stories of success and explicitly link them with supportive environments. However, positive stories and encouraging examples are not enough. All those concerned with change must emphasise the *business* case for diversity. Relating LGBT diversity and inclusion to economic gain is ultimately the biggest driver of change.

I have known Martin Sorrell, the chief executive of WPP, the multinational advertising and public relations firm, for more than two decades. I know that he believes in LGBT equality on a personal level. But, as a shrewd businessman, he also understands the practicalities of promoting LGBT inclusion to the companies he advises. 'The commercial power of the gay community is sufficient to make people think carefully about opening their mouths, and once they do open their mouths, to do the right thing,' he says. 'I feel we are in a better place.'[61]

THE BENEFITS OF COMING OUT

FOR ME, THE process of coming out happened in reverse. In an ideal world, I would have built up the confidence to tell my friends and colleagues about my sexual orientation. This should have happened away from the cameras and on my own terms. Then, advised by BP's press relations team, I would have managed my own public disclosure.

Instead, the newspapers exposed me. Only in the aftermath of that ordeal did I begin to build up my inner strength, aided by friends and others. While the circumstances were not desirable, they turned out to be a blessing in disguise. Aspects of my life that I had kept separate for a long time finally came together, and I was able to live openly with my partner. Psychologists would say my dissociated selves had merged into a single, complete person. I put it more simply: my life got easier.

Years later, I am still asked whether I could have risen to the position of CEO if I had come out earlier in my career. The answer is that I do not know. I always found an excuse not to reveal the truth. I believed that coming out would be socially and professionally unacceptable. I will never know if that was true.

The paranoia of life in the closet unsettles people inside it and clouds their judgement. It leads them to exaggerate beyond reason instances of homophobic banter or prejudice. It also leads to overly complex analysis and preparation for the perfect moment to come out professionally: perhaps when they get the next promotion, when the media is otherwise occupied, when there is the perfect public event or when they have been living in a committed relationship and can show their straight colleagues that their lives are not so different.

This is short-sighted. Personal circumstances may change, but there will never be a convenient time to come out. Dr Siri Harrison, a clinical psychologist in London, works with closeted men and women in the financial services industry. She sees a common pattern in her patients who are ready, but unwilling, to come out at work. 'It's almost as if people are waiting for a time when they won't have anxiety and worry, and won't feel awkward,' she says. 'That's not likely to happen.'[1] Because gay men and women are part of a traditionally marginalised group, 'the process of coming out will usually elicit anxiety and fear.' These emotions are by-products of change and uncertainty.

Gay men and women contemplating coming out must do so in their own time, and they must feel comfortable and safe about their decision. At the same time, it is important to be realistic. It is not possible to avoid uncomfortable feelings. Coming out, however, will make it possible to overcome them.

'ISN'T THAT UNFORTUNATE?'

GROWING UP IN the suburbs of New York in the 1970s and 1980s, Mike Feldman did not have any gay role models. 'There was no *Will & Grace* or *Ellen*, and people were always making negative comments about gay people and HIV,' he says. Once, when he was eleven years old, a pair of gay men sat down near Feldman's family in a restaurant. 'My mother said, "Isn't that unfortunate?"' he remembers. 'She was so innocent and didn't know anything about homosexuality. That one comment stuck with me for a long time.'[2]

By the early 1990s, when Feldman was in his early twenties and working at Hewlett-Packard in Maryland, colleagues were making more pointed remarks. He remembers an instance when a colleague described a trip to California. 'It's incredible,' he said on his return. 'Everybody is gay and wearing shorts to work.'

Those statements were insensitive, but they were not hostile. Feldman stored them anyway, and spent the first fifteen years of his career at Hewlett-Packard in the closet. At the time, he justified his secrecy by saying to himself that his personal life had nothing to do with how he did his job. Looking back, he believes a fear of rejection underscored his decision, which had a profound impact on his daily life. He refused to discuss his personal life with colleagues and was evasive when responding to questions. He would frequently go on business trips and colleagues would ask him who was looking after his golden retriever. Rather than telling them that his long-term partner would be at home, he said that a friend would take care of the dog. In his effort to deflect attention away from his own life, he did not ask others about theirs.

Colleagues began to view him in one of two ways. Some saw him as one-dimensional and boring, a 'career nut who only cared about climbing the ladder'. Others, who suspected that he might be gay, pitied him for being uncomfortable in his own skin. That fostered distrust. 'They were thinking, "If he's hiding this, maybe he's hiding other things too,"' he says. 'It was a bad situation all around and I wasn't building personal relationships.'

In 2001, he came out to his family. They were immediately accepting. In 2004, his company moved from one building to another, and his secretary somehow secured him a corner office, despite the fact that he was only a director and those offices were reserved for more senior executives. To celebrate he took her out to dinner. A few days later, she upbraided him for sending her home from his apartment early. '"You knew I had a crush on you and led me on,"' she said. 'I didn't want her to be hurt so I said, '"Paige, I'm gay!" and she said, "Thank God!"' She was relieved that it was not a personal slight.

Having an authentic relationship with his secretary was a good start. The next turning point came when the head of Feldman's division presented a quarterly report to employees. It covered the financial results and the company's other activities, which included becoming a major corporate sponsor of Out & Equal Workplace Advocates, the LGBT workplace equality organisation. 'I had never seen the word "gay" on a PowerPoint slide,' he remembers. 'This man reported to the CEO, was of Indian descent and did so many visible things for the LGBT community. I was sitting there ashamed.'

Feldman had cultivated a good working relationship with his line manager over two decades. But his manager's conservatism made him nervous. Feldman intended to tell him in person, but he could not summon up the confidence. He sent his boss an email instead. 'I just said, "I believe it's time for me to come out of the closet. It's time for me to be more of a role model."'

His boss responded four hours later. He was clear that Feldman's disclosure would make no difference to his standing in the company, and that he still valued his contributions to the team. He also asked for some feedback: he wanted to know why Feldman had waited so long to tell him that he was gay and had a partner, and asked whether he had done or said anything to make him feel uncomfortable. 'Now I feel less guilty when you're travelling,' his boss wrote, 'because I know someone is there to take care of your dog.'

Coming out by email or letter provides an important buffer. On the one hand, it allows the individual coming out to adjust to the significance of what they have done without having to deal immediately with any adverse reaction. It also allows the person receiving the news, particularly someone who might struggle with it, to experience their full range of emotions in private.

For face-to-face encounters, particularly those that may provoke anxiety, Dr Harrison advises patients to draft a list of two to three talking points. These talking points can be as simple as "I am gay" and "I cannot change this".' Harrison believes that this helps her clients remain clear-headed without 'falling prey' to the potential negative reaction of others. He or she must allow the person to whom they are speaking to react in their own way and sometimes badly. If either party needs to leave, then they should. Their new relationship does not need to be settled immediately. 'Challenging conversations can turn into a whirlwind and it becomes so complicated that the person coming out cannot think,' Harrison says. 'They may stutter or feel like they are revealing too many details or not revealing enough. When initially coming out, keep it simple so that you can take care of yourself in the situation.'

Feldman did not experience any hostile conversations. Rather than telling his staff directly, he dropped references to his partner in conversation. 'They were just thankful that I had finally said it,' he says. By tearing down those barriers he started to form more meaningful personal relationships. He was also promoted three more times at Hewlett-Packard. Feelings of vulnerability and anxiousness gave way to a sense of control and empowerment, and the desire to be out in all aspects of his life.

In 2013, he went for a job interview with the chief executive of Xerox and five members of that company's executive team. In each of those interviews he mentioned his partner. 'I did that because I wanted to test their reaction,' he says. 'I wanted to know if this was a place that valued diversity, and a place that I wanted to join. They were all very comfortable and at ease with me having a partner.' He accepted a role as senior vice president a few weeks later. Within six months he was promoted to president.

'WE ALL STRUGGLE DIFFERENTLY'

BY JUNE 2011, the global media had already heralded Beth Brooke as one of the world's most successful businesswomen. She started working at Ernst & Young in 1981, left briefly to join the Treasury Department under President Bill Clinton and returned to the accounting firm ultimately to become the global vice chair of public policy, overseeing the firm's policy operations in 140 countries. Along the way, she championed women's issues through the World Economic Forum and United Nations, and on six separate occasions *Forbes* magazine had named her one of the world's 100 most powerful women. In spite of all the accolades and recognition, she feared 'being defined as being anything other than a great professional and a great leader'.[3] The fifty-two-year-old did not want to be known as a lesbian.

Earlier in her career, Brooke had been married to a man for thirteen years. Being a divorcee had always given her a natural cover. 'It was pretty far into my career that I had to start thinking, "I am actually leading a gay lifestyle and now

I'm hiding it,"' she says.[4] Even so, she viewed her private life as private, and did not believe the act of hiding had any impact on her performance.

In February 2011, the leader of Beyond, EY's LGBT employee resource group, asked Brooke to appear in a campaign video for the Trevor Project, an organisation that works to prevent suicide among youth who are or who think they may be lesbian, gay, bisexual or transgender. LGBT employees from EY would speak briefly in the video about how their lives had improved since coming out. Brooke remembers sitting on a plane and reading her part of the script, which was written for her as a straight supporter. 'I thought, "How can I be inauthentic?" I'm talking to kids who might be sitting at home thinking of killing themselves and I'm actually going to say something not authentic. I wasn't going to do that.' She rewrote her part. The next day, she handed the teleprompter technician her new script, which included these lines: 'I walked in your shoes. I'm gay, and I struggled with that for many years. We all struggle differently, but we all struggle.'

The video would not come out until a month later, the morning after Brooke was to accept an award from the Trevor Project on behalf of EY. Given her position at the organisation, she notified a small number of colleagues to let them know she would be coming out. In her acceptance speech, she talked about her role in the video. At some point she said 'as a leader who is gay' and the crowd rose to give her a five-minute standing ovation. She stopped speaking and wept. 'In my mind, I was a coward and a hypocrite for having been closeted for fifty-two years of my life, and thirty-one years of my work life,' she now says. 'Since most of that audience was gay or gay friendly, I expected a reaction of, "Well, where have you been? Why are you just getting around to saying this now?" I learned that the whole gay community was so respectful that this was uniquely personal. Every person comes out in their own time, in their own terms.'

POSTER CHILD FOR DIVERSITY

GIVEN THE COMPLEX and personal nature of coming out, there are no firm rules that apply to everyone and across all circumstances. Coming out in London might mean the risk of embarrassment, homophobic comments or damage to corporate relationships; in Moscow or Kampala, it means the risk of physical reprisals and public shaming.

For closeted employees in relatively supportive environments, however, the consequences of coming out are rarely as bad as they expect. 'People need to get out of the victim mentality,' says Antonio Simoes, a senior banker at HSBC.[5] In his view, 'Most people, at least in countries like the UK, need to realise that this bogeyman issue is in their minds and not necessarily around them.'[6]

Simoes has been openly gay since the summer of 2000, when he was an associate at Goldman Sachs in London. In the years it took him to climb from an associate to his present position, he has come to regard his sexual orientation as an asset. He came out to Goldman's human resources department while discussing accommodation for him and his partner in London that summer. The company had several openly gay employees among support staff, but there were no out investment bankers that Simoes can remember. 'All of a sudden I was the poster child of diversity in banking,' he says. 'I would be wheeled out at business school diversity events. The logic of the companies on campus seemed to be, "Look how cool and diverse we are."' The presence of big firms at LGBT recruiting events furthered his belief that being out was the right decision. Companies were not only open to gay employees: they were actively courting them too.

As his career progressed, Simoes's decision to be open about his sexuality worked in his favour in at least three ways. First, revealing his sexual orientation boosted his personal reputation. Coming out can be perceived negatively, so 'people thought I was smart enough and good enough that I didn't need to care about any negative consequence'. Second, by the time Simoes became a team leader at the consulting firm McKinsey & Co., employees attached a 'cool factor' to him being out. He was the only partner who was out in the London office and became the executive sponsor of the employee resource group GLAM (Gays and Lesbians at McKinsey). 'My now-husband went with me to all of the events, so I was clearly out,' he says. It helped colleagues see Simoes as relaxed and approachable, which made for smoother interactions.

Finally, Simoes believes his authenticity breaks down barriers with colleagues. 'People trust me more because I'm reasonably forthcoming about something that is not always easy for other people,' he says. Some leaders talk about their five-year-old child and their wife. Simoes talks about his husband and their dog. 'The moment you avoid a question when someone asks about your wife, you feel somewhat ashamed,' he says. 'You don't feel good about yourself and that shows.'

I know that closeted employees frequently believe that coming out will prevent them from reaching the top. Simoes appears to shatter that myth. For decades, banking has been regarded as being populated with sharp-elbowed aggressive men. But the world has moved on and it has brought the banking sector with it. 'Being homophobic is no longer acceptable,' he says of the younger generation. 'It's the other way around. Most bankers I know go out of their way to show how cool they are with my sexuality.'

I used to think that the higher I rose within BP, the more dangerous it would be to come out, because my ascent was accompanied by a rapidly expanding public profile. I now realise that the opposite is true. 'At some point, if you're not truthful about certain elements of your personal life it becomes a huge liability,' Simoes says. 'There is no such thing as "My private life is my private life" and "My professional life is my professional life". People won't trust you and may even use it against you.'

Lesbians report similar experiences. Carole Cameron oversees more than 170 employees as a senior manager of mechanical engineering at the aerospace giant Lockheed Martin in Sunnyvale, California. When she joined the firm in the early 1990s, friends at the corporation suggested that she remove the rainbow stickers from her truck and go into hiding for fear of reprisals. But she says that she did not have the energy to go into the closet. Instead, she made no changes to her appearance and went to work in men's clothing. She has been promoted six times. 'Perhaps there's pressure to be a better performer when you're openly gay,' she says. 'If I were just an average performer, maybe I would be discriminated against.'[7]

Psychological studies suggest that a majority of people associate homosexuality with gay men rather than lesbians.[8] As such, stereotypes and stigmas attached to homosexuals may stick to gay men more than lesbians. Heterosexual men appear to socialise more easily with lesbians than with gay men.[9] Although it may not apply to all lesbians, Cameron believes that being out in a male-dominated industry has actually helped her build relationships with heterosexual men at work. 'All my life, straight men have loved to confide in me,' she says. 'They feel very safe. Many won't tell other men how they think or feel because of rivalry and pressure. And they don't want to talk to straight women because of potential attraction.'

Coming out also puts up a barrier to unwanted sexual advances. Julia Hoggett of Bank of America Merrill Lynch describes it this way: 'When some, but by no means all, men interact with women in the workplace, there can be the sense that they're trying to determine if they are a secretary, a colleague or a potential girlfriend,' she says. 'That's what happens when you get groups of people working together in almost any environment, particularly one that demands the long hours of this profession. The great benefit of being openly gay is that that question never comes up. So your relationship with your male colleagues is businesslike from the start. My relations with male colleagues are often easier, more straightforward and genuinely ones of friendship because there is no issue there. In a bizarre way, I feel that being openly gay has actually made life easier rather than harder.'[10]

It can also make it easier to get a foot in the door. Rumour has it that a small but growing number of straight business school students are posing as LGBT candidates to recruiters to exploit what they perceive as a positive advantage for gays. Ivan Massow, the entrepreneur who was at the forefront of developing the LGBT market for financial services in the UK, understands why this might be the case. 'There are more road shows for gay students and applicants,' he says. 'There are more invitations for them to go to the Goldman Sachs LGBT day where they can meet a partner of the firm. They go, flirt with a nice man who's probably gay and score a much quicker sense of kinship. They strike up a relationship, are remembered and have the right to phone them back or send an email following up. All these things are much harder if you come from the bland wash and are competing alongside all the other boys and girls. It's an advantage as you go through.'[11]

TRANSGENDER TABOO

IN 2002, MARK Stumpp was the chief investment officer of Quantitative Management Associates, a subsidiary of Prudential Financial in Newark, New Jersey. Stumpp oversaw thirty-five employees and $32 billion on behalf of client pension funds and investors. One day, while discussing research with the co-founder of the firm, Stumpp, then forty-nine, revealed that he would be undergoing surgery to become Maggie. His boss smiled, but was clearly shocked by the news. 'He said, "Maggie, we love you and whatever you want to do will be fine,"' Stumpp says. 'Then he ran out of the door like the *Road Runner* cartoon and went to a bar. I didn't see him for the rest of the day.'[12]

That awkward conversation was the culmination of a lifetime of worry. From the time Stumpp was a child, she had wanted to be a girl. She attended a Catholic school and her parents caught her cross-dressing when she was in the third grade. They did not discuss it. As she matured, Stumpp would go to libraries in search of literature on her condition, only to find that there was none. In the early 1980s, therapists told Stumpp that she was not transgender, but rather a gay man in denial. However, over time she began to see herself in transgender role models like Renée Richards, the tennis player, and Jan Morris, the historian and travel writer.

Accepting her situation was not the same as confronting it. 'The subject was so taboo that if you brought it up you'd be considered a raving lunatic,' she says. Most of the stories she had heard of transgender employees transitioning at work had ended with them being dismissed. Stumpp made a pact with herself. She would earn as much money as she could, and would change sex after retiring from Prudential. In the meantime, she would have to live with her personal dissatisfaction and distress. The terrorist attacks on the World Trade Center on September 11, 2001 altered her view of the matter. 'People woke up that morning, went to work and didn't come home,' she says. 'I changed my trajectory. What I planned to do after I retired became something that I would do as quickly as possible.'

Stumpp had low expectations for her future. At best, she imagined that bosses would keep her around for five more years before quietly pushing her out. They were open-minded, but would have little choice. The investment management business depends on trust. 'No one is going to give you hundreds of millions of dollars to invest if they have questions about your stability,' she says. 'I was very concerned that our clients might view us as a risky enterprise if the chief investment officer was going through this kind of personal change.'

With that in mind, Stumpp decided to treat her transition as a business issue. A few days after her conversation with the co-founder, she drew up a plan for her colleagues. She proposed stepping back from the client-facing side of the business, and would instead conduct more research. Spelling out how to move forward put senior colleagues at ease. When Stumpp left for several weeks to undergo surgery, the co-founder of the firm called everyone on Stumpp's team to explain her transition. He paved the way for her return while she sat in hospital recovering.

Stumpp's transition was unique not only because of her

status within the firm. At the time, the vast majority of transgender employees would leave their job, transition to their new sex and then resurface in a new location with a new identity. Stumpp's transition would affect not only her but her colleagues too.

Unlike bisexual, gay and lesbian employees, she could not come out overnight. Stumpp had to work with the legal and marketing teams to change her name on regulatory documents and mutual fund prospectuses. And because the investment management business is highly regulated, she had to inform all clients about her transition. The vast majority did not care. They were happy that Stumpp had made their money grow, and saw no reason to switch firms because of changes in her personal life. A few clients did ask to meet with her. 'They wanted to look me in the eye and make sure that I hadn't gone over the deep edge,' she says.

Perhaps the biggest test came when a large institutional investor asked to meet before renewing their arrangement. 'They didn't want to meet me in their offices because they were afraid I'd look like a truck driver in a dress,' she recalls. So Stumpp met with them in a steakhouse. When she arrived, the table of men began drinking immediately. After several rounds of drinks, it was obvious that they still had a rapport, even if Stumpp wore a dress rather than a suit. 'After a few rounds of drinks, the guy next to me leaned over and said, "You know, for a guy you don't look so bad." We all had a good time and the relationship continued.'

It also prospered. Over the next ten years, the value of assets under Stumpp's management grew from $32 billion to more than $100 billion. Clients could have moved their investments elsewhere, but money continued to flow into the firm. 'This throws light on the idea that transitioning will put business at risk or make customers uncomfortable,' says Stumpp, who is now a senior advisor at Prudential. 'Whenever I met with institutional investors, they wanted to know what we were working on. The whole trans issue wasn't even a footnote.'

NOT EVERYONE IS HETEROSEXUAL

IT IS CLEAR to me that a major reason LGBT employees remain closeted is the fear of offending their colleagues. A 2009 report from the Human Rights Campaign found that half of the employees surveyed who were not out said that they worry that coming out will make people feel uncomfortable.[13] Twenty-five per cent believed that co-workers would view disclosure of sexual orientation or gender identity as unprofessional, and two-thirds of them said that their sexual orientation 'is nobody's business'.[14] The fear of putting off friends and colleagues prevents many LGBT people from being authentic in all circumstances. Whenever they deflect questions about their personal life or obscure important details about themselves, they sacrifice their own comfort for the comfort of others.

It is unfortunate that they feel this way; I used to feel the same way too. Discussing homosexuality still raises eyebrows in a way that discussing heterosexuality does not. Heterosexuals declare their own sexual orientation more frequently than many realise. They do so by discussing their husbands and wives, by displaying wedding pictures in their office and by showing up to work events with their partners. People do not think of sexual orientation when Jeff talks about his wife Anne. But when Mike talks about his partner Luke, some of the same people may think that Mike is unnecessarily discussing his sexuality.

That sort of thinking arises from the assumption that by default everyone is heterosexual. Coming out will never be a one-off event. One of the benefits of being in the public eye is that you rarely need to come out more than once. However, most openly gay employees must come out again and again, when they meet new clients or co-workers, or change jobs.

It is important to fight the temptation to go back in the closet. Hoggett follows a simple rule: if a colleague or client outs himself as a heterosexual, she outs herself as a lesbian. 'When someone says to me, "My wife is a bit grumpy because we got home and the kids were filthy after soccer," I'll explain my own circumstances, and that I have similar experiences with my family,' she says. 'You occasionally encounter someone who says, "Why did you tell me that?" I say, "Because you said the same thing to me." Often the people I am talking to have never thought about it in those terms, but I believe that for most gay people that's how it feels.'[15]

Hoggett acts with conviction and confidence. She is not asking for someone's approval, just as a straight man is not asking for approval when he discusses his wife. She is merely sharing information. Just as her straight colleagues have photos of their children on their screensavers and desk, so does she. It can spark a conversation about her family circumstances with strangers. Sexual orientation is not merely about sex. It is about how and with whom people build their lives. This approach means that gay employees can take control of their identity. Rather than cowering in fear of discovery, they share information about their private lives on their own terms.

Rosalyn Taylor O'Neale is a diversity consultant in New York City. She believes that it is her responsibility to create a sense of safety for LGBT people in every setting where she operates. She always mentions her wife in her first conversation with a new client or colleague, so that they 'have the opportunity to digest that there are women who have wives and men who have husbands'.[16]

She does not care if she sounds like a militant campaigner. Her commitment to being out stems from at least two experiences. The first is growing up in the 1950s in the southern United States, where public restrooms were still segregated by race. One of her aunts 'passed as white'. She would only allow O'Neale and her mother to visit her after dark, so that the neighbours would not see African Americans entering her house. The same fear of being outed as black kept her from attending her own sister's funeral. 'When you tell one lie, you have to tell another lie, and you end up telling so many other lies it is crazy,' she says. 'I realised that I never wanted to "pass" for anything that I wasn't. I could never do that about race, and I wasn't going to do that about sexual orientation.'

The second experience occurred in the late 1980s, when she was interviewed for a job overseeing diversity work. O'Neale arrived at the interview wearing a three-piece trouser suit with a man's tie and sporting a short afro. 'I had on everything but a T-shirt that said, "I'm a lesbian", so I assumed she understood that,' she says. Shortly after starting her job and outing herself to her co-workers, she encountered trouble with her boss. 'She began to talk about my performance and it quickly went to "'I'm going to fire you"',' she remembers. That woman was the head of the company's affirmative action programme. 'The message was clear: it's OK for you to do "valuing differences" work as a black person, but not as a lesbian.' O'Neale went on to have a successful career. Her boss, who turned out to be in the closet herself, did not.

It often feels risky, but O'Neale comes out in nearly every situation. She recalls teaching a course on unconscious bias for a major international company in Milan. When she entered the room, the audience saw that she was black, they heard that she was American and they saw that she was a woman. Someone asked her when she had arrived in the country. 'Now I have to come out,' she said to herself. In a matter of seconds, she assessed the situation, weighed the consequences and recognised that there was no threat to her safety. 'I say, "My wife and I arrived on Tuesday."' She makes similar calculations when she meets new clients and when she is sitting next to someone on a plane. She prefers to know where she stands with someone, regardless of the consequences: 'Have I lost clients because of that? Yes. Am I OK with that? Absolutely.'

Coming out in client relationships is not always about risk: it is also about opportunity. Claudia Brind-Woody, the vice president and managing director for intellectual property licensing at IBM, has experienced this first-hand. 'I've had client relationships where I've come out, trust increased and the deal got done quicker,' she says. 'In any negotiation, trust is a fundamental value.'[17]

She says that her staff need to reflect the real world in order to serve it. If a business assumes that all of its clients are straight, it will be wrong between 5 and 10 per cent of the time. She recounts a gay colleague's experience with a long-term client. As the business relationship developed, the client's representative, a man, began discussing personal matters such as children and hobbies. 'Our gay sales guy was struggling with whether he should come out,' she says. 'He finally worked up the courage to do that. He came out to his client and the guy said, "Really? Me too. Can we quit going to football and go to the theatre instead?"'

EVEN IN JAPAN

I FIRST WORKED with Miranda Curtis when we co-chaired a meeting of business executives and the UK's Prime Minister, David Cameron. It was clear to me that she was an experienced businessperson. Over the past two decades, she had built and managed international partnerships for Liberty Media, the world's largest international broadband cable group. She travelled from her home in London to Tokyo at least once a month, overseeing the set-up and eventual sale of J:Com, Japan's largest broadband cable operator. Liberty sold its stake in the firm for $4 billion in 2010.

Curtis has always taken an understated approach to her sexual orientation, both at home and abroad. She does not lead with that information, but she does not lie when asked. In Japan, she spent countless hours sitting at dinner with her colleagues, but the nature of Japanese business discouraged any discussion of spouses or partners. Businessmen in Japan tend to talk about their children, their hobbies and their pets. They rarely mention their wives. In that context, Curtis often discussed the herd of alpacas she and her partner reared in the English countryside. 'I talked about my partner and they took that to mean the person who looked after the alpacas,' she says.[18]

Eventually the issue came to a head. Around the time they were taking the company public, her colleagues scheduled their annual general meeting at a particularly inconvenient time. It would coincide with Curtis's civil partnership ceremony and a celebratory vacation. It was the first meeting that Curtis had ever missed. She did not explain why. The following trip she sat at dinner with Japanese colleagues, who clearly had her absence on their minds. 'They looked at me and said, "Miranda-san, you're wearing a ring. Is this a significant ring?"' Curtis said yes. 'And is this a happy significant ring?' She said it was. They did not ask if she had been 'married' and the context was clear. So was the sincerity of their response: 'We are very pleased.'

That quiet acceptance emboldened Curtis to tell her senior advisor, who was in his early seventies at the time. She invited him and his wife to dinner with her partner, who was visiting Tokyo. He asked if the woman coming was Curtis's life partner. 'I said "yes",' she remembers. 'He said he would be honoured and delighted.' He and his wife later visited Curtis and her partner at their farm in the English countryside.

The manner in which people approach their sexual orientation publicly will reflect the range of personalities within the LGBT universe. Some people, like Curtis, are relatively private. Others are far more forthright. The important point is that people must feel comfortable and secure in their approach. Even if you are more guarded, you can still demonstrate confidence in yourself. 'I never denied who I am, but I have not made my sexuality the primary element of what I present to my business colleagues,' Curtis says. 'They think of me as a competent colleague who was a good member of the team. If you can get those messages across, then after that your personal life is much less of an issue.'

STEREOTYPES

FOR DECADES, I believed that it would be socially unacceptable to come out. I worried that the negative stereotype of a gay person would overshadow the reality of who I was. I am sure that staying in the closet did prevent some people from forming unflattering opinions about me. However, I am no longer convinced that they matter.

By avoiding one stereotype, I conformed to another: that of a gay man in the closet. I had a dominant mother and a high-powered job. I associated almost exclusively with straight people and I worked more than I lived. Every moment of my day, from getting up in the morning to going to bed at night, was scheduled, often months in advance.

Observant people, and there are many at BP, would have seen me for what I was: a gay man too fearful to come out, a man who poured himself into work to escape personal frustration and loneliness.

In retrospect, I know that the people who matter to me did not care whether I was gay. But they felt for me for carrying such a heavy burden, even if they did not always know precisely what it was. During a recent business trip to San Francisco, I spoke to Gini Savage, a long-standing friend who sensed my inner turmoil decades ago. 'You were an incredibly reserved person,' she remembers. 'No one knew where they could put a foot down with you because you were very private.'[19] She and others had to tread carefully. We danced around the subject of my sexual orientation without ever confronting it. It was tiring, and not just for me.

As chief executive of BP there was so much to do. I was able to keep myself occupied and to channel my frustration into growing the business. But you can only divert the tension and anxiety for so long. Towards the end of my tenure, I felt those negative feelings turning back on me. Had I stayed in the closet, I think I would have remained an incomplete and unfulfilled person. Since I have come out, my friendships, both old and new, have flourished. And so has the relationship with my partner, whom I respect and admire. These are the greatest joys in my life. Without them life would remain incomplete.

Coming out does not mean your life will be peace and serenity. You will still encounter people who make you uncomfortable. You will still have to make difficult decisions. You will still face challenges big and small, meaningful and trivial. However, as I have learned since coming out, you will be better able to cope with all of them.

CHAPTER SEVEN

OPINION FORMERS AND ICONS

DAVID SHELLEY, THE group publisher at Little, Brown in London, has never been in the closet at work. He struggles to recall any difficulties created by his sexual orientation. To the best of his knowledge, he has never been denied a promotion because he is gay. He has never heard homophobic banter in the office, and his colleagues have never been embarrassed to ask him details about his personal life. He has built a success-ful career in which he has been entrusted to work with some of the world's best-selling authors, including J. K. Rowling. 'I've been in the industry for fifteen years and I can't think of a bad reaction,' he says. 'Actually, there isn't a reaction at all. It's seen as such a normal part of life.'[1]

The publishing sector appears to be remarkably accepting of people's sexual orientation; Shelley's experience is not unique. In 2013, of the handful of openly gay UK chief executives or chairmen, two were the heads of major book retailers.[2]

Openly gay men have served as editors of GQ, *New York* and *New Republic* magazines in the US. The newspaper industry is considered more conservative. However, Guy Black, who is openly gay and the executive director of the Telegraph Media Group in London, says, 'I know senior gay people in most of the newspaper environments in this country and I cannot detect any anti-gay attitudes or hostility. I just don't think it's an issue any more.'[3]

The same appears to be true within the world of digital media. In 2004, Thomas Gensemer co-founded Blue State Digital. In the run-up to the 2008 US presidential campaign, it spearheaded Barack Obama's digital media strategy, which was unprecedented in both its size and scope. Gensemer was out from the beginning. He says that digital start-ups are filled with young people, who help foster a tolerant environment. 'It leads to transparency and a more casual workplace,' he says. 'It used to be that people would stay in the closet because they thought it would limit their careers. Today the opposite is true. Being in the closet becomes a question of character.'[4]

In the publishing and media sectors, the sexual orientation of employees is no longer considered remarkable, nor is it considered an indicator of someone's potential. The wide-spread acceptance that gay men and lesbians experience within this sector has two consequences. First, it boosts their representation because gay people feel comfortable entering the sector. Second, it discourages gay people from suppress-ing who they are. They see other successful gay people and are comfortable to come out. That critical mass of openly gay employees is the beginning of a virtuous circle.

When it comes to diversity and inclusion, the media is a unique part of the corporate world. But in many sectors of business and in many other parts of society, old-fashioned attitudes remain entrenched. The struggles and successes of LGBT employees elsewhere may offer lessons for gay people in business.

Sport, politics and the law are particularly instructive. They offer people an unparalleled platform from which to influence public opinion or set public policy. In order for society to become inclusive and accepting, it is essential that these sectors set an example and embrace those who differ from the norm.

Professional sport and politics represent opposite ends of the spectrum. Sport is one of the few sectors that lag behind business in the representation of LGBT people. Homophobia is perceived to be endemic, more so in team-based sports than those involving individual athletes. Just as a business unit works towards a common goal, so does a sports team. One player's homosexuality may be seen as a barrier to cohesion. Politics, on the other hand, has experienced radical progress over the past three decades. The public increasingly accepts gay politicians, so long as they are honest about their sexuality. Progress has come at every level, and in some surprising places.

POLITICS

IN 2012, WHEN Justin Chenette stood for election to the Maine House of Representatives, he was a twenty-one-year-old college student. He knew that in other electoral races throughout the country opponents were using sexual orientation as an electoral issue. He also knew that gay marriage would be on the election ballot, and that it might stoke homophobic rhetoric. Even so, he never contemplated staying in the closet. 'I came to the realisation that I just need to be upfront,' he says. 'I think it's better to control the message rather than let the message control you.'[5]

As the election approached, vandals moved his election posters to more prominent positions in town and sprayed them with the word 'gay'. In response he remained silent. He won 60 per cent of the vote and became the youngest publicly elected, openly gay official in the US. Being out may have put a few obstacles in his way, but he believes openness was a more effective strategy than hiding. 'The idea of trust is so important in politics and business,' he says. 'If you can't be trusted because you're withholding information, people are going to sense that.'

When I was coming of age, I am sure that it would have been impossible for an openly gay person, of any age, to secure public office. Today, Chenette's election is yet another sign that progress has come to politics at every level. From the UK to Poland, and from the US to Italy, gay men and women are achieving public office in increasing numbers. In the US, there are more than half a million elected positions, from school board member to president. In 1991, LGBT people occupied just forty-nine of those positions. By October 2013, that number had increased by a factor of eleven.[6] Progress is happening at the highest level. In 2003, there were just three openly gay members of Congress. Ten years later, there were seven LGB members, including Wisconsin's Tammy Baldwin, the first openly gay senator, and Kyrsten Sinema, the first openly bisexual congresswoman.[7] Iceland and Belgium have appointed gay prime ministers; Germany has appointed a gay foreign minister; and even more surprisingly, Rosario Crocetta became the first openly gay governor of Sicily. He won partly because of his reputation for cracking down on the Mafia when he was the mayor of a small coastal town. Speaking to *The Washington Post*, he admitted that he was an unlikely choice. 'I'm homosexual, which I call a gift from God, and no, I didn't hide it one bit!' he said. 'The fact that I'm here is almost inconceivable.'[8] National legislatures from Canada to Ireland to New Zealand have welcomed more LGBT members in recent years than ever before.[9]

At the end of 1996, there was only one openly gay member of the UK's House of Commons. However, by the end of 2013 there were twenty-four,[10] equivalent to 3.5 per cent of the chamber.[11] That is a remarkable turnaround.

However, progress has not been even. In 2010, senior government minister David Laws resigned after he was found to have contravened the spirit of the law governing accommodation expenses, so that he could keep his relationship with another man secret.[12] In an echo of my own story, Laws's desire to remain in the closet cost him his job.[13]

Politics is built on trust. Gaining the trust of the electorate is easier when politicians present themselves authentically. In the short run, hiding one's sexual orientation may offer a degree of comfort for those uncomfortable with coming out publicly. In the long term, the revelation that a public figure has been hiding his or her sexual orientation is potentially more damaging than having acknowledged it from the start. To be successful, politicians must position themselves not as the gay candidate but as the candidate who happens to be gay. Voters are not preoccupied with sexual orientation.

Klaus Wowereit, who became mayor of Berlin in 2001, understood that long before he stood for the city's top office. Elected to the city council in 1995, he came out step by step as he rose through the ranks of city politics. In this process, he slowly informed his colleagues and important journalists. He therefore avoided a dramatic moment of revelation. 'I think a "slow outing" strategy is a good way to go,' he says. 'You're not covering anything up, but you're not making a lot of noise about it either. In the end, word got around and everyone knew.'[14]

However, circumstances forced the pace. In June 2001, the majority of the public did not know that Wowereit, a member of Germany's Social Democratic Party (SPD), was gay. He had unexpectedly been appointed acting mayor after the city's coalition government collapsed. As city elections approached in October, the polls suggested he was the front-runner. 'I had to decide how I was going to deal with my homosexuality,' he says. 'What I really think is that it's my own business. On the other hand, being forcibly outed by the tabloids seemed like the worst of all options. If I didn't want to be put under pressure, I needed to go on the offensive.'

Wowereit told his party that he was gay and warned that his sexuality could become an issue in the election. Eventually, the media learned about his talk with his own party and reporters began hounding him. 'I said to myself, "This is your life, you haven't done anything wrong and you don't have to justify yourself. They aren't going to beat you that way."' He decided to speak openly at a party convention in Berlin, declaring, *'Ich bin schwul, und das ist auch gut so.'* The phrase, which is translated as 'I'm gay, and that's okay', became a popular rallying cry across the country.

Wowereit's opponents did attempt to use his sexuality to undermine his credibility. The mayoral candidate for the conservative Christian Democratic Union said that Wowereit demonstrated 'deformed character' and suggested that his sexuality would limit his authority, particularly on matters related to the family.[15] That rhetoric was not sufficient to dissuade voters. In handing victory to Wowereit, they embraced or at least overlooked his sexual orientation. As he says, 'People want to see results and aren't that interested in my private life.'

Chris Smith, now the head of the UK's Environment Agency, tells a similarly optimistic story. He came out in 1984, a year after being elected to the UK Parliament. The social climate of the mid-eighties did not encourage others to follow his lead. Shortly after he came out, a British tabloid mocked him in a cartoon that depicted someone in drag standing in the House of Commons. In 1987, the offices of *Capital Gay*, a free gay newspaper, were firebombed and Elaine Kellett-Bowman, a conservative MP, defended the action. 'I am quite prepared to affirm that it is quite right that there should be an intolerance of evil,' she told the House of Commons.[16] In the following spring, Margaret Thatcher's government passed a Local Government Act, Section 28 of which defined gay partnerships as 'pretended family relationships'. All of this occurred against the backdrop of the AIDS epidemic. It is therefore hardly surprising that Smith remained the only openly gay Member of Parliament for thirteen years.

During this period, Smith managed to increase his majority enormously and in 1997 Tony Blair appointed him to his Cabinet, making Smith the first openly gay minister in UK history. His appointment caused barely a stir. Gay people with aspirations in politics and business should take away three points from Smith's success. The most obvious one is that gay people can be just as effective as straight people in leadership roles. The second is that the press quickly grows tired of covering your sexual orientation once you have revealed it. And the third is that your personal and professional relationships will remain strong even after you have come out. 'You can be openly gay and get overwhelming acceptance from everyone that you deal with, whether it's the general public or fellow politicians,' Smith says. 'It makes no difference to the relationships that you're going to build up with them.'[17] In 2013, the Conservative MP Crispin Blunt proved Smith's point when he successfully defeated a campaign to de-select him as the local candidate for his constituency, after he came out and left his wife of two decades. He won the selection ballot by a margin of five to one, defeating, in the words of his supporters, the 'dinosaurs' who sought to have him removed.[18]

The changes that have taken place in the UK over the course of my lifetime are remarkable, but they should not blind us to the realities elsewhere. The challenge for LGBT politicians in conservative countries remains immense. In Poland, for example, only around 40 per cent of the population believe that society should accept homosexuality.[19] In recent years, more than 60 per cent of Poles believed that same-sex couples should not have the right to live their lives openly, and less than one-third of the population supported gay marriage.[20] But in 2013, when Lech Walesa, the godfather of Polish democracy and Nobel Peace Prize Laureate, said that gay men and women have no right to sit on the front benches of parliament and if elected should sit 'behind a wall', senior politicians and figures in public life expressed outrage.[21]

In 2011, two candidates made history when they became the first LGBT politicians to win seats in the Polish parliament. Robert Biedroń, the first openly gay Polish parliamentarian, and Anna Grodzka, the first transgender Polish parliamentarian, stood for election as members of the newly formed Palikot Party, which campaigns for greater respect for diversity. In a surprise result, the party became Poland's third most popular. I suspect generational change is helping broaden minds. So too is the interconnectedness of Europe. Young Poles who study and work abroad in the EU are likely to be returning home with more progressive values.

While societal change has enabled LGBT politicians to be elected, it does not shield them from prejudice. Inside parliament, Grodzka has had to cope with transphobic reactions to her election. 'Sometimes I am left with a sense of disbelief at the brutality and primitivism of attacks on me by certain politicians on the right,' she says.[22] The best example of this involves Krystyna Pawlowicz, a member of the Law and Justice Party. In public interviews, she has compared Grodzka to a horse, among other things. 'What kind of woman is she? She has a face like a boxer,' she said in an interview with

Polish media. 'Just because you stuff yourself with hormones, it does not make you a woman.'[23]

In spite of the ignorance displayed by people like Pawlowicz, it is clear to me that Grodzka and other LGBT politicians in Europe and the US have opportunities today that they did not have even a decade ago. State representative Justin Chenette has the following advice. 'Your sexuality isn't a choice, but your openness about it is,' he says. 'You can choose to live in the closet, but it's going to eat away at you. At the end of the day, you're not going to be effective.'[24]

SPORT

IT IS IMPOSSIBLE to know how many gay men and women have reached the upper echelons of business. I am certain, however, that many of them have risen to senior positions without being out. Business appears to be much more progressive than professional sport. The majority of professional sports teams around the world do not contain a single openly gay player. Philipp Lahm, a straight soccer player in the German Bundesliga, has spoken out against homophobia in sport. 'Sure, politicians can now come out as homosexuals. But they don't have to play in front of 60,000 spectators week after week,' he said in an interview. 'I don't think society is far ahead enough that it can accept homosexual players as something normal, as in other areas.'[25]

It may be fair to assume that many gay people decide not to pursue professional sports. A majority of those who do pursue a sports career choose to remain closeted. When National Basketball Association (NBA) player Jason Collins came out in April 2013, he became the first active player across the four largest American sports leagues ever to do so.[26]

A similar situation prevails in Europe. By the end of 2013, there was no single openly gay player in the top six national soccer leagues.[27] In February 2013, Robbie Rogers, an American who played with Leeds United, came out by announcing his homosexuality on his blog. He retired in the same announcement, later explaining that he feared the reaction of soccer fans and media. He resumed his career with the Los Angeles Galaxy three months later. Justin Fashanu, the only other high-profile professional soccer player ever to come out in the UK, committed suicide in 1998.

Coming out can be seen as disruptive to the unity of a team. In the late 1970s, Glenn Burke, a former baseball player for the Los Angeles Dodgers, was known to be gay by his teammates. In 1995, he died of complications related to AIDS. Before his death, he told the Associated Press that homophobia was rife during his four years in Major League Baseball. He claimed that once, after management decided not to renew his contract, his manager stood in front of the team in the dugout, stared at him and said, 'I don't want no [sic] faggot on my team.' He also alleged that a coach once offered to pay for his honeymoon if he would only marry a woman. When he refused, he was traded to another team.[28]

Decades after Burke's experiences, some closeted players might still worry about the impact that coming out will have on team cohesion. In August 2013, my partner and I visited some long-standing friends of mine at their house in the English countryside. We arrived for afternoon tea. Among the guests was a man in his early thirties who was introduced to us as Thomas, a footballer from Germany. After tea, he took a walk with both of us in the garden. In those most unlikely surroundings, he then described how, during the latter part of a twelve-year career in professional football, he dealt with the realisation that he was gay.

By the time we met, he had reached the point of having to decide whether to retire from professional football. A long career playing for various clubs in the German Bundesliga, Italy's Serie A, the English Premier League and the German national team meant that injuries were a factor. But he was also preoccupied with whether to come out and when. He was very interested in my story and the circumstances surrounding my outing. He wanted me to describe the fears I had and how my life had changed.

Less than three weeks later, the Hammer, as he was known for his powerful left foot, officially hung up his boots. Thomas Hitzlsperger announced his retirement at the beginning of September 2013.

Thomas visited us in London in December, and debunked some of the conventional wisdom about homosexuality in football. 'Most people talk about the reaction of the fans, but everything is controlled, and the stadium is full of cameras. What could actually happen to me?' he says. 'And I didn't really have a problem with gay jokes among the players – some of them are funny – but homophobia is more difficult to deal with. I think though that if I had come out, some players would have supported me, and others would have followed.'[29]

Even though it comes from the world of football, in which openly gay players and former players are so rare, Thomas's story is like so many others in this book. It was my strong impression that, like many in business, he was worried that a poor performance could have been blamed on his sexuality. And in a story familiar to minorities throughout history, Thomas seems to have held himself to a higher standard in order to avoid public attention that might have revealed his sexuality.

In the few conversations I had with Thomas, I suggested to him that there is never a good time to come out, nor a bad time. We also discussed the positive impact that his coming out would have on the younger generation of footballers, and his desire to encourage a public debate about homosexuality in sport.

Within a week of our interview, Thomas had taken the decision to come out. On 8 January 2014, he disclosed his sexual orientation in an interview with Germany's *Die Zeit* newspaper. 'I'm coming out about my homosexuality because I want to move the discussion about homosexuality among professional sportspeople forward,' he said.[30] Reaction from the media and fellow players was swift and overwhelmingly supportive, as with this Twitter message from English footballer Joey Barton: 'Thomas Hitzlsperger has shown a lot of courage today. Sad times when people have to wait till they retire from their chosen profession before they feel other people will judge them solely on who the human being is. Shame on all of us as a society.'[31]

It remains to be seen whether Hitzlsperger's action encourages an active player to come out. In the past, coming out adversely affected the overall appeal and commercial attractiveness of a player. This was a factor in keeping them in the closet. Athletes typically have a narrow window of only a few years in which to make a living. Coming out could threaten opportunities for sponsorship, as was the case with Billie Jean King thirty years ago. By 1981, she had already won twelve Grand Slam singles titles in tennis and was one of the world's most prominent female athletes. That year, her former secretary Marilyn Barnett, with whom she began a relationship in the early 1970s, had filed a lawsuit, which made King's sexual orientation public. Against the advice of her counsellors, King staged a press conference and confirmed that she had indeed had a relationship with Barnett. Her sponsors made what seemed to be an economically rational decision, underpinned by homophobia. Within one day she had lost all of her sponsorships, which she says amounted to at least $2 million.[32]

Martina Navratilova, who won a record nine Wimbledon singles titles, admitted that she was a lesbian a few months after Billie Jean King's announcement. She was ranked number two in the world at the time and had an enormously high profile after fleeing Communist Czechoslovakia and becoming a US citizen. 'I didn't lose any deals because I didn't have anything outside of tennis to begin with,' she says over the phone from her home in Florida. 'I started winning all those Wimbledon titles and deals still didn't come my way. I know I lost a lot of money and recognition for coming out, but money never came into my decision to do so.'[33]

Throughout the 1980s, Navratilova faced hostility from the media; at that time, she largely attributed this to the fact that she had emigrated from a Communist country during the Cold War. Before a tournament in Amelia Island, Florida, a local columnist described her match with Chris Evert, the blonde, heterosexual American, as a match of 'Good vs Evil'. Later, a male sportswriter asked her, 'Are you still a lesbian?' She responded with a question of her own. 'Are you still the alternative?'[34] Fans reacted badly to her presence. 'People never say anything to your face, but I certainly felt it in group settings when I would walk on to the court. Everybody was clapping for Chris, but then people were whistling and jeering at me. I was like, "What exactly did I do to deserve you booing me?"'[35] It is only in retrospect that she realises how much of that stemmed from homophobia.

These stories show the immense difficulties associated with being openly gay in professional sport. Athletes can decide either not to pursue their sport professionally, or to do so in the closet. It is impossible to know which path more gay athletes have chosen. For example, the number of openly gay athletes competing at the 2012 Summer Olympics was 0.16 per cent of the nearly 15,000 participants; this is unlikely to represent the true number of gay athletes.[36] A third option, coming out and competing, appears to be the least likely choice.

Professional sport has immense power to influence all parts of society. It must become more representative. It must not foster discrimination, which is exactly what it does at present. However, attitudes appear to be changing in line with those of the public. The risk of being alienated by sponsors, teammates and professional sports bodies has declined. Corporations now see opportunity in sponsoring gay athletes. In April 2013, Nike signed its first-ever deal with an openly gay athlete, Brittney Griner. Jason Collins came out a few days later. Nike, which had previously struck a deal with him, issued a statement of support. 'We admire Jason's courage and are proud that he is a Nike athlete,' it said. 'Nike believes in a level playing field where an athlete's sexual orientation is not a consideration.'[37] Public support came from a number of other celebrities and athletes, including the commissioner of the NBA David Stern and fellow player Kobe Bryant.

A growing number of heterosexual players are now promoting acceptance of gay athletes. 'There's gay players and we've played with gay players and you've seen gay players come out post career,' Brendon Ayanbadejo formerly of the Baltimore Ravens said in a 2013 radio interview, after filing an amicus brief with the Supreme Court in support of gay marriage. 'So we're just slowly progressing every day, every month, every year to players being comfortable to be themselves. If they can be themselves, they can be better players.'[38] The English Football Association has taken action too. In

2012, the body disciplined a player for using a gay slur on Twitter. In 2013, Liverpool Football Club initiated a ban on those slurs. That autumn, some players began wearing rainbow laces in support of LGBT players.

Billie Jean King believes that changing attitudes in business are influencing those in professional sports. 'When an athlete like Jason Collins came out, he got congratulated by the President of the United States. When I was outed, I lost all of my endorsements overnight,' she says in an email to me. 'The business community in general is much more receptive to gay and lesbian athletes today. Any person who comes out should be allowed to do so on their own terms – at a time when they are ready to live their truth. I didn't have that opportunity and I paid the price. But that was then and this is now.'[39]

Increasingly, gay athletes understand that momentum is on their side. Thomas Hitzlsperger believes that there is a growing expectation that management support gay players if they come out. 'It becomes a political question for the teams you've played for, a test of how they handle it,' he says.[40]

Late in 2013, British Olympic diver Tom Daley revealed that he was in a relationship with a man.[41] He joined the ranks of Mathew Helm, Matthew Mitcham and Greg Louganis, three other Olympic medal-winning divers who had come out previously. The BBC telephoned me to ask me to give a brief interview immediately following his announcement. In that interview, I said that coming out is never risk free.[42] However, it was my hope that Daley's honesty would lead to a positive outcome for him and would show others what is possible. The support he received was tremendous. Later that day, Gary Lineker, one of the UK's most famous soccer broadcasters and former players, sent a message of support via Twitter. The comedian Stephen Fry put the event in perspective when he sent his own message that said, 'I opened the second door on my advent calendar and Tom Daley came out. Seriously @TomDaley1994 congratulations. So happy for you.'

Today, the line between professional sport and business is blurred, and experiences are now overlapping. Rick Welts became one of the highest-ranking executives in the NBA. Welts, who grew up in Seattle, started working as a ball boy for the Seattle Supersonics basketball team in 1969, returning to them after completing university, and rising to be their director of public relations. By 1982, he was living in New York with a gay architect whom his colleagues had never met. He avoided talking about his partner because of his fears about coming out. 'There had never been a person in my shoes,' he says. 'I couldn't learn from their experience or gain confidence, and I had no idea what would transpire.'[43]

His partner died in 1994. Welts was so closeted then that he took only two days off to mourn. He returned to the office completely numb and could not share his grief with anyone. By 2009, he was living in Phoenix and was the chief executive of the Phoenix Suns basketball team. A second, nine-year relationship ended badly. 'A major factor in the breakdown of that relationship was the fact I could not have the most important person in my life involved in my work life,' he says. 'At that juncture, I decided that if I was going to have a successful relationship in the future I couldn't do it the same way. I was going to have to be much more open about my life.'

In May 2011, Welts decided to come out in a front-page interview with *The New York Times*.[44] As part of the process, the journalist writing the story interviewed David Stern, the man who had nurtured Welts's career. Stern said that he had known Welts was gay for years, but that he never discussed it with him because he did not want to intrude.

'I had expected 90 per cent of letters to be positive and 10 per cent to be negative,' he says. 'But thousands of people sought me out through email, and I received dozens and dozens of handwritten letters. There was not a single person who had a negative word to say. It doesn't sound credible.' Welts's experience accords with my own. Like him, I received an overwhelming number of supportive letters and emails. Just one person took the time to write something negative.

Shortly after coming out, Welts moved to San Francisco to join his new partner. In September, the Golden State Warriors named Welts their new president and chief operating officer.

LAW

IN 2002, ADRIAN Fulford was appointed to the High Court Bench. One year later, he became one of eighteen judges to be appointed to the new International Criminal Court. In 2012, he joined the Court of Appeal, the second-most senior court in England and Wales. These were all important appointments, but also unlikely ones. Fulford did not attend Oxford or Cambridge University. He studied history, rather than law, and in his words, 'not very well'.[45] His pupillage was not in one of the more traditional law offices. Perhaps most limiting of all, he was openly gay from the late 1970s.

Fulford's decision to come out was not without consequence. He received cold shoulders from some of his fellow barristers, and dealt with judges who, on occasion, would take 'a hard, uncompromising, unfriendly stance', which he could only interpret as homophobia.[46] In 1994, when he originally applied to become a part-time judge, he endured a hostile interrogation by a panel of 'men in grey suits', who asked him, 'Do you really have to pursue this?'

In spite of the pervading attitude from parts of the judiciary, Fulford was promoted to the bench. He believes that he would not have been successful without the presence of an open-minded Lord Chancellor, who was responsible for his application being considered on its merits rather than on his sexual orientation. As in business, leadership from the top can make all the difference. Senior judges and lawyers whose prejudices reflected another era eventually retired, and in the years that followed, others have shaken up the judiciary. As Fulford completed a training course to become a judge, he remembers that one of his instructors, a distinguished judge who subsequently became the Lord Chief Justice of England and Wales, reassured him that there was no glass ceiling for gay people and that it made no difference to him in assessing aspiring judges. Role models like that have, Fulford says, moved the judiciary beyond 'the private fiefdom of a very narrow kind of white heterosexual male'.[47]

The judiciary is not yet representative of society as a whole. But the diversity among today's young lawyers should change that in the future, providing people remain vigilant about discrimination. 'Obviously, there might be particular sets of chambers, or particular firms of solicitors in various parts of the country, where the old ways still apply,' Fulford says. 'But, as a generalisation, I feel that the windows have been opened and a very strong wind has blown through, sweeping away most of the regrettable aspects of the past. If a young barrister asked me whether they should come out, I would say, "Fear not. Absolutely fear not." Look what has happened to me.'[48]

Many gay men and women now think that they would face fewer difficulties in the legal profession than they would in business. I can think of two important reasons why this may be the case. First, education tends to be positively correlated with an understanding of diversity, and a career in law requires a lengthy and rigorous period of study. And second, the practice of law requires impartial analysis to be applied on a daily basis, forcing out unfounded value judgements.

However, a recent study surveying some employees in the UK legal profession found that only one in four lesbians and only one in ten gay men were fully out in their law firms.[49] For those lawyers who do come out, it is usually a matter of going it alone. Less than half report that they have an openly LGBT colleague whom they would consider a role model.

Daniel Winterfeldt, a partner at CMS Cameron McKenna, began working in London in 1998. At his first law firm, he was the only openly gay lawyer among a staff of 500. Five years later, when he moved to another firm, he was once again the only openly gay lawyer. At times that dulled his ambition. 'I didn't look up and think that there was a role for me further down the line,' he says. 'I had worked really hard to make these opportunities happen for myself, but, bizarrely, I just felt lucky to have a job.'[50]

It may be that the number of LGBT lawyers is less important to law firms than the number of women and ethnic minorities. The intake of male and female lawyers is largely balanced. However, women account for less than 10 per cent of all equity partners at the UK's 100 leading law firms.[51] Ethnic minorities account for just 5 per cent of partners.[52] Law firms may have taken a practical view that they should focus their diversity and inclusion efforts on these groups, which outnumber the LGBT population.

In spite of the lack of role models, young lawyers are coming out more often than their predecessors. Of people aged fifty-one to fifty-five, only 15 per cent felt comfortable being out at their first firm. For lawyers under twenty-five years old, four times as many did.[53] Older people derive their views from a different period, when overt harassment or discrimination were more common. Younger people who have come of age in a more tolerant world have different experiences. It is obvious that they are more confident and comfortable with themselves. Whether they will enjoy equal advancement and promotion remains to be seen.

In 2008, Winterfeldt established the InterLaw Diversity Forum, an informal network of LGBT lawyers in the UK. By the end of 2013, the group had more than twelve hundred lawyers from seventy law firms and forty corporations. It has become a resource for the many lawyers who lack openly gay colleagues. Aided by the InterLaw forum, the legal sector in the UK has made great strides. In 2009, no law firms were ranked among the Top 100 employers in Stonewall's annual Workplace Equality Index. By 2014, that number had risen to ten.

Corporate clients are pushing law firms to expand their diversity and inclusion efforts beyond women and ethnic minorities. Lawyers perceive them as more progressive and more attuned to LGBT staff. Steve Wardlaw, an openly gay partner who runs the London office of Baker Botts, has been out since the 1980s. He says, 'I think the legal profession has been more old-fashioned. It's a matter of "Don't frighten the horses."'[54] Reinforcing this, Winterfeldt says that 'management in law firms are finally waking up and realising that there is a real issue here. They are watching talent walk out the door to their clients.'

ICONS

POLITICS, SPORTS AND the legal profession are in different phases of their journey to inclusion. The pace of progress may vary, but the direction is the same. This is important because these sectors, combined with the entertainment sector, are able to produce the people who can most significantly shape public opinion and public policy. These role models can become some of the most important gay icons in society. They will also powerfully influence business attitudes.

Although progress and obstacles vary, I do believe there is one universal principle applicable to any field. Put simply, change requires leadership. As we will see in the next chapter, this is guided by practical activity.

CHAPTER EIGHT

SHATTERING THE GLASS

WHEN IT COMES to social change, governments can nudge and legislate, but they cannot deliver. Only individuals, on their own and as members of society's institutions, can implement change. Out of all the institutions that shape our lives, businesses are designed to solve problems and deliver solutions. It is therefore obvious that, with a combination of effective individual leadership and practical measures, businesses can shatter the glass closet.

This book's journey provides the context for action. Many companies are now making it possible for LGBT people to feel included. But from my experience, they now need to do two things uniformly and consistently: they need to set a clear direction; then they need to attend to the tools of management that make it possible for that direction to be implemented.

Enacting policies for LGBT people is a natural starting point on the road to inclusion. Their real-life application can be measured and provides insight into the basic values of a company. But there is a difference between the security that these policies are designed to provide and the safety and comfort actually experienced by LGBT employees. Although a company's leadership may embrace LGBT employees, it is not always obvious to prospective applicants, new recruits and closeted employees. As I know from decades of hiding my sexual orientation, closeted people usually assume that coming out will have dire consequences. Companies must demonstrate with words and deeds that this is a fallacious assumption.

In 2006, Peter Murray left his job as an advisor in the UK Parliament to take on a role at Arup, an engineering consulting firm. 'A senior politician said to me, "Be very careful. You're joining an engineering firm and these guys will be less open to people being out in the workplace,"' he says. That well-meaning but misguided advice compelled Murray to spend two years hiding details of his personal life from senior management, and made him very sensitive about revealing his sexual orientation. 'The problem was a lack of signposts that indicated Arup was a gay-friendly employer. My bosses took it for granted that people already knew that.'[1]

If coming out were not such a daunting thought to LGBT employees, then more people would have already done so. There are hurdles stopping them. Some are deeply personal and a company alone cannot remove those. However, companies can create the right signposts. They must move to establish cultures of inclusion codified not merely in policies and handbooks but also in the thoughts and behaviour of employees. This begins with corporate leaders. They must think about inclusion in every decision that they make. They must consider whether they are open to new ideas, understand people as individuals and care about each member on their team.

To get LGBT inclusion right, there are seven actions to take:

- actively set direction from the top
- create and support LGBT resource groups
- encourage straight allies
- set concrete goals and measure against them

- get LGBT people to accept individual responsibility
- identify role models and tell their stories repeatedly, and
- set clear expectations for those working in conservative countries

ACTIVE LEADERSHIP

ON THE DAY the US Supreme Court overturned the Defense of Marriage Act, some of the world's biggest corporations rushed to issue statements in support of the decision. 'This is good for our company and clients, but more importantly, it's the right thing to do,' Jamie Dimon, the chairman, president and CEO of JPMorgan Chase, said in a statement. 'The rights of all people are important and must be protected.' Mark Zuckerberg, the co-founder and CEO of Facebook, posted a message of support on his Facebook page: 'I'm proud that our country is moving in the right direction, and I'm happy for so many of my friends and their families.' In a speech in December 2013, Tim Cook, CEO of Apple, expressed the company's 'support [for] legislation that demands equality and non-discrimination for all employees, no matter who you love'.[2]

These examples illustrate a fundamental premise of inclusion: leadership must set a clear direction. This begins with policies that ensure LGBT people are treated equally. There can be no overt or subtle discrimination, and no tolerance for any sort of homophobia.

Positive statements from the senior leadership can set a precedent for managers throughout the organisation. Antonio Simoes of HSBC regularly speaks about gay issues in public and at in-house events. 'People underestimate how important it is for leaders in general to talk about LGBT inclusion,' he says. 'If you live in London, New York or even Hong

Kong, which are diverse and open, you may not think you need to talk about it. But even in the UK there will be someone in our 50,000 workforce who may feel out of place. If you say it is OK to be different, then they will feel empowered. It's amazing the number of people who email me from HSBC around the world to say, "I thought your speech was really motivational and I feel really excited about working for a bank that truly values diversity and meritocracy."'[3]

Chief executives who take LGBT inclusion seriously make time to broadcast their beliefs. In 2012, the organisers of Out on the Street, an annual LGBT leadership event, brought together a large number of senior executives from eleven organisations to discuss LGBT inclusion on Wall Street. It marked the first time that serving CEOs of US banks, including Bank of America Merrill Lynch and Goldman Sachs, came together in one place in support of LGBT equality.[4] Subsequent meetings around the world attracted even more chief executives and senior leaders from banking, accounting and related services.

In November 2012, I moderated a panel at one of these meetings. It was clear to me that speakers were preaching to the converted. My long-time friend and former BP colleague Paul Reed spoke at that meeting. He thinks that there are two benefits from doing this. First, speakers can share best practices with each other, and second, their comments are reported publicly. That news finds its way back to employees at the firms represented at the event. Comments that Paul made at the summit were published in *The Times* of London, and then reprinted in the *London Evening Standard* and *Gay Star News*. 'There were hundreds of people at BP who saw it and I got a lot of internal mail as a result,' he says. 'The publicity really helped promote the acceptability within BP of coming out.'[5]

Fine speeches do not create sustainable actions, but without the right direction from the top, nothing will happen. The seriousness with which a leader approaches diversity and inclusion is also reflected in an organisation's structure. Today, about 60 per cent of Fortune 500 corporations have a chief diversity officer or another executive role that oversees diversity and inclusion.[6] The higher a company ranks on the Fortune 500 list, the more likely it is to have such a role.[7] Giving an executive title to the manager accountable for diversity and inclusion elevates the status of the position, and sends a strong message that diversity matters. In 2000, I hired Patti Bellinger to steer BP's diversity and inclusion efforts, and gave her the title of Group Vice President. That made her one of only forty group vice presidents in the entire company of over a hundred thousand employees. To make her role significant, it was important to give her a title of significance.

Of course, titles are meaningless if a manager does not have the ear of the company's top executives. In the US, just one-quarter of managers responsible for diversity and inclusion reports directly to the CEO, while the majority reports to another department, usually human resources.[8] This is rarely effective. 'If you report to the head of HR, there is a perception that you are attacking the very things that that person has upheld,' Bellinger says. 'You want to change individuals and win hearts and minds. But you also need to effect systemic change, and sometimes that means undoing or revising existing HR processes, which may present discriminatory obstacles.'[9]

Whilst human resources serve a core business function, it is not always viewed as critical to the mission of the corporation. Trevor Phillips, the former chairman of the UK's Equality and Human Rights Commission, believes that reality squeezes out efforts to improve diversity and inclusion. 'The responsibility for driving change shouldn't be parked in HR,' he says. 'Where it should really be is sales and marketing.'[10] In order to compel change, leaders must cast diversity and inclusion as a *business* issue, not as an ancillary function. At BP, I cared about diversity and inclusion on the human level. But I also saw its absence as a threat to productivity and creativity. Bellinger began her time at BP working in the human resources department, but soon she was given free reign and worked across ethics, legal compliance, marketing and recruitment. The deputy chief executive directed her work, not the head of human resources.

When a chief executive views an issue as important, he or she inevitably mobilises the 'usual suspects', those in the inner circle who can be trusted to get things done. Although Bellinger reported to my deputy, she and I were in regular communication. This was obvious to everyone. In the few instances in which she had problems with a stubborn executive, she knew she could force action by saying, 'Shall we talk to John about this?' The tone from the top made it clear that we were serious about diversity.

Leadership must behave consistently with its policies, even when dealing with external suppliers. Most significant and successful companies ask that their values of safety, honesty and treatment of staff be adopted by their suppliers in order to be eligible for business. Corporations must make sure that these suppliers' internal rules reflect their own policies towards LGBT staff too, otherwise a firm risks compromising its values and diluting its message of inclusion.

For instance, IBM's supplier guidelines state that their suppliers must not discriminate on the basis of sexual orientation, gender identity or expression, and make clear that the corporation will not tolerate any harassment or variations in pay, benefits or promotion for LGBT staff.[11] Standing up to clients is not always easy, but there are examples of firms that do. Claudia Brind-Woody is determined that IBM will not put business above its values. 'In the past, we've had clients who didn't want black or female sales reps,' she explains. 'We said, "Well, fine. We won't send any. In fact, we won't send anybody because we don't want you as a client."'[12]

LGBT RESOURCE GROUPS

THE TONE FROM the chief executive should cascade down through the corporation's top executives and the leaders of each business unit, but often it does not. Communication is rarely as effective as it ought to be. It may not get through the middle ranks of management who are preoccupied with the urgent, day-to-day tasks of business. LGBT resource groups, whose leaders make the time to deal with inclusion issues, can help spread the message.

The activities of LGBT groups are varied and creative. At the Campbell Soup Company, the LGBT group OPEN has staged a photo day where all employees, straight and gay alike, are encouraged to bring in photos of their families. That gives employees a natural and non-threatening way of disclosing their sexual orientation. At the Houston office of BP, the LGBT group once brought cupcakes along with kitchen magnets that, in an inspired variation of 'Bring your kids to work!', read, 'Bring yourself to work!'

In 2012, the LGBT resource group at Goldman Sachs, London, chose bisexuality as a theme for its activities that year. They invited a bisexual film-maker to premier his documentary film about bisexuality at their offices, as a part of Pride Month activities in June, and followed this with a panel discussion on the topic. The event was open to all employees based in Goldman Sachs's London offices. 'As a network, we have been keen to make sure that we are as embracing and supportive as possible of each of the different groups within the LGBT network,' says Gavin Wills, managing director and co-head of the Goldman Sachs EMEA LGBT Network. 'The documentary film was a terrific vehicle to help people understand the perspectives of bisexual people and open up the topic for wider discussion.'[13]

At Google, gay employees call themselves 'Gayglers' and large numbers of them attend gay pride parades, from San Francisco to Dublin to Bangalore. In 2012, they marched in the New York City parade behind a double-decker bus with a rainbow flag painted on its side. A video about Google's LGBT resource group shows employees from their global offices, including Warsaw, Tel Aviv and Singapore, talking about how easy it is to be different at the company. 'I'm transsexual and I transitioned right here at Google,' says Tammy, an employee from the Mountain View, California, office. 'I'm extremely proud to work in a place where not only can I say, "I'm transgender," but where the most common response was, "Cool! Tell us more."'[14] Joao, an employee at the São Paulo office, says he feels completely safe turning up to work on a Monday 'and talking about how my weekend went, if I travelled with my boyfriend or went to a restaurant where gays usually go'.

STRAIGHT ALLIES

IN ALL LIKELIHOOD, the tone is set from the top by a hetero-sexual person. Renee Brown of Wells Fargo, a large US bank, says that 'straight, active allies' are the most effective advocates for gay staff. 'It's the straight people who are married that can start changing people's perspectives,' she says. 'They may have kids, close friends or relatives who are LGBT, and they have a passion around this and feel it's important to educate and share. Change happens when straight people are with us.'[15] Chris Crespo, EY inclusiveness director, says straight colleagues are crucial to the activity of their resource group Beyond. 'When we did our last survey of the group mailing list, we found that 58 per cent of people were actually straight allies,' she says.[16]

Senior leaders should create and participate in formal 'allies programmes' that encourage straight employees to give their support for LGBT inclusion. At Accenture, a global consulting firm, employees place supportive banners in the footer of their emails, while at Goldman Sachs, supporters set up 'ally tents' on their desks. The tents measure three by two inches and are decorated with a rainbow. Placards have also been displayed at companies such as Alcoa, Barclays and Dell. At the headquarters of Walmart, supportive executives wear pins with the Walmart logo and a rainbow.[17]

Bank of America Merrill Lynch launched its allies programme in June 2013. More than two thousand staff signed up in the first five months. A package arrives to welcome them and explains how they can 'help people in the coming-out process'. They also receive stickers, posters and a list of prominent champions of gay people. This includes business leaders such as Meg Whitman of Hewlett-Packard and Jeff Bezos of Amazon, and entertainment figures such as Lady Gaga and Bruce Springsteen. There is a list of ten tips on how to talk with their straight colleagues about their experiences with LGBT friends and family members, how to offer mentorship to LGBT employees and how to challenge homophobic or insensitive behaviour.

Homophobic jibes are an obvious example of what is not acceptable. Even in an environment with all the appropriate policies, a bad joke or anti-gay slur can generate a fear of exclusion or disadvantage. Straight leadership and committed supporters must respond to these situations without compromise.

Insensitive behaviour is not limited to pejorative language. It extends to so-called 'micro-inequalities', actions and behaviours that assume that everyone is heterosexual or suggest heterosexuality is superior to homosexuality. Examples are assuming that every man is married to a woman or the practice of not asking gay people about their partners in order not to make them uncomfortable, while asking straight colleagues about theirs. Programmes like Bank of America Merryl Lynch's are designed to make people sensitive to these issues. Deborah Dagit, the former chief diversity officer at Merck, refers to her husband publicly as her partner so that members of the LGBTA (the 'a' stands for straight allies) community know she is a supporter. 'Being an inclusive ally does not require a lot of effort, courage or creativity,' she says. 'It simply necessitates being conscious that words matter – and then choosing words that reflect your intent to accept.'[18]

GOALS AND MEASUREMENT

FOR DECADES, EMPLOYERS have understood the value of tracking the career progression of women and ethnic minorities. Data help companies to identify problems in hiring, promotion and performance. Over time, data can help managers determine whether their efforts have had an impact, and how best to refine and improve their processes.

Employers are beginning to extend their diversity monitoring to sexual orientation and gender identity. According to the Human Rights Campaign's 2014 CEI, almost half of the 734 employers rated in the US allowed employees to disclose, in an anonymous or confidential manner, their sexual orientation and gender identity.[19] That percentage is up from just 16 per cent in 2006.[20]

Since 2008, EY has asked employees to disclose their sexual orientation in its biannual survey, which measures engagement and job satisfaction. 'Unless you have the ability to count the effect that you're having through an HR process, nothing will get done around it,' says Chris Crespo. 'At EY, we are exploring the use of our Global People Survey data to be able to see results and trends in headcount, job satisfaction and engagement.'[21]

Selisse Berry, the founding chief executive officer of Out & Equal Workplace Advocates, headquartered in San Francisco, says that corporations need to be patient when collecting this sensitive information. 'The first time you put self-ID in place, many people, especially people who are closeted, will have heart palpitations and say, "I'm not going to out myself,"' she says. 'The second year they will see it and have less of a reaction. And by the third year, they may actually tick the box.'[22]

Taking all steps necessary to protect the confidentiality of these reports and explaining why management is interested in them are the best ways to boost response rates. When JPMorgan conducted its first anonymous Global Employee Opinion Survey, 2 per cent of respondents identified themselves as LGBT. For its second survey, the company did not allow employees to remain anonymous, but management stressed that responses would be kept confidential. The proportion identifying itself as LGBT nearly doubled to 4 per cent.[23] Self-identification is a key benchmark of progress.

INDIVIDUAL RESPONSIBILITY

THE LEADERSHIP OF an organisation has a responsibility to stick to its commitments. But the responsibility to build an inclusive environment is not theirs alone. Change does not happen unless individuals take responsibility themselves.

In 2003, Chris Crespo started asking colleagues at EY to discuss LGBT issues. At the time, the firm did not have a resource group for LGBT staff. However, around forty people at all levels, and from around the country, began participating in informal discussions about their concerns and being out in the workplace. During one group phone call, it emerged that Mike Syers was the only senior partner taking part. Crespo asked whether he would use his position to help her coordinate the launch of the professional network Beyond. Syers sought advice from friends and colleagues outside the firm. 'The advice I received was, "You are new to the company. You don't really know where this is going to go. Why do you want to pigeonhole and label yourself?"' The discussions in which Syers had participated persuaded him otherwise. He knew that some gay employees felt uncomfortable being out in the workplace. 'It wasn't about me,' he says. 'It was really about creating a platform to move things forward. It was because of meeting people like Chris and others who were passionate and committed that I decided to get involved.'[24]

Syers and Crespo then scheduled a meeting with John Ferraro, the company's senior vice chair and later its global chief operating officer. Ferraro was open to learning more about the discomfort some employees felt at work. 'We sat down and took out pictures of our kids,' Syers remembers. 'I have one daughter and Chris has triplets, and we just talked and we started to get to know John.' Ferraro immediately offered his support and Beyond was born shortly thereafter.

In 2005, the firm became the first of the Big Four accounting firms in the US to achieve a perfect score on the CEI, an achievement it has repeated every year since. As Syers and Crespo know, you have to ask in order to receive. They must be encouraged to participate in identifying challenges and initiating solutions to create an inclusive environment. Then they must take their careers into their own hands. 'The firm cared, they supported us and we felt as though we could make a difference,' Syers says. 'We have had many very senior leaders in our firm as allies since day one.'

ROLE MODELS AND THEIR STORIES

ONLY IN COMBINATION with world-class leadership will the changes described in this chapter have a chance of making a lasting difference. That begins with a clear and consistent tone from the top. I was not the first senior executive to make speeches about the importance of diversity and inclusion only to remain in the closet myself, and I know that I was not the last. If company policies and speeches are seen as tokenistic or even hypocritical, gay people looking for the right signals from their leadership will only find confusion. That is a recipe for inertia.

Tone from the top must be accompanied by stories that make the issue real. Employees who have come out should talk about their experiences, because there is nothing more effective than real-life examples at dispelling fears. Senior management should hold them up as role models, examples of excellence to be lauded and emulated by those who are not yet bringing their whole selves to work. Company policies and LGBT networks create the right space to come out, but role models prove that success is possible. They provide an inspiration and an aspiration for closeted employees.

Ben Summerskill, the chief executive of the UK-based lesbian, gay and bisexual equality organisation Stonewall, believes that is essential for any business serious about recruiting and retaining top talent. 'One way in which the labour market has changed dramatically in recent years is that young people, particularly graduate recruits, are starting to say to businesses, "You talk a lot about diversity, but you need to demonstrate it to me,"' he says. 'The only way you demonstrate to a young gay person – or a young black person or a young woman – that your business will support their career development is if you can point to people like them at the top of the business too.'[25]

Those successes must be celebrated, but it is just as important to identify failures. Being honest about where things have gone wrong is a critical step in gaining the trust of employees who are thinking about coming out. It is not appropriate to project only success; some stories must be told of disaffected and badly treated employees.

From the courageous politician to the successful LGBT network, and from national programmes of persecution to individual examples of homophobia at work, stories of success and failure must be repeated again and again. In my experience, that is the only way to embed change in an organisation.

WORKING IN
CONSERVATIVE COUNTRIES

While there has been great progress in many countries, over one-third of all countries in the world still criminalised homosexuality at the end of 2013. Jonathan Cooper, chief executive of the Human Dignity Trust, is working to repeal these laws. 'In these countries, gay people are subject not only to risk of arrest, detention and prosecution but also exploitation, extortion and degradation,' he says. 'It can take the form of low-level humiliation, as when police make gay men clean an officer's car, but it can also be more serious, as when police fail to investigate serious crimes because the victim is gay. Gay men and lesbians effectively become outlaws.'[26]

For LGBT employees working in these countries, the challenges are more daunting than those in liberal enclaves like New York and London. The role of LGBT resource groups for these workers is even more important.

BGLAD, the gay and lesbian group at consulting firm Bain & Company, organises a conference for its members every year. They bring LGBT staff from around the world together for several days of events. To outsiders, it may look like a retreat, but the events allow staff from smaller offices to know there are people like them thriving within the organisation. 'It has the biggest impact on our colleagues from India, China and Dubai,' says Chris Farmer, a member based in London. 'They have rarely seen a group of LGBT people of that size together and comfortable in themselves. It has become their biggest support network.'[27] The support continues year round on the group's email list. It connects members with hundreds of other LGBT people to whom they can turn for advice.

Having an 'allies group' that incorporates heterosexual staff is particularly important in conservative countries. It allows companies to expand their LGBT diversity initiatives to places where LGBT organisations are traditionally under-represented. The presence of heterosexuals in the group makes them less controversial. It also allows LGBT people to join these groups without actually coming out.[28] 'We launched our India LGBT Network in 2009,' says Stephen Golden, head of the Goldman Sachs Office of Global Leadership and Diversity for Asia Pacific. 'Since then, we have seen our network grow to over 300 employees, including "out" LGBT professionals and straight allies.'[29]

Companies that are most committed to LGBT diversity will not bend their policies, even in the most challenging environments. IBM, for instance, does not allow its non-discrimination policy to be adjusted in any of the 170 countries where it operates, including those in Africa and the Middle East. It goes further than the legal requirements of many countries by prohibiting discrimination and harassment based on sexual orientation. That sends a strong message to governments, who understand the importance of major international companies for job creation and the local economy. 'We want our LGBT employees to be able to have international assignments like anybody else as they develop their careers,' says Brind-Woody. 'We really focus on safety within the walls of IBM.'[30]

LGBT employees posted to conservative countries do not live their lives entirely within the office. They can be out within the walls of their company, but they must be mindful of the dangers that may greet them in business settings and on the street. It is crucial that employees and the managers encouraging them to go abroad have frank discussions about the potential challenges and dangers they may face. Employees will do their own research, but at a minimum the company must supply up-to-date information about the legal status of LGBT people in specific countries and explain the risks. In some instances, the company will struggle to have a same-sex partner recognised as such. For instance, Stonewall, the UK gay and lesbian advocacy group, encourages companies to include special emergency protocols for gay staff in homophobic countries. As it explains: 'Gay staff may need health insurance that enables them to be flown back to the UK or a third country for treatment with their partner, since a normal incident such as a road traffic accident could leave a gay staff member exposed to discrimination at a time when they are very vulnerable.'[31]

Gay employees must never be coerced into accepting a difficult posting. Nor should they be made to feel that declining one may hurt their long-term career. At international law firm Simmons & Simmons, employees can speak confidentially with staff in human resources without disclosing their sexual orientation. They can then negotiate alternative assignments or the number of return visits to their home country or even the possibility of working remotely.[32]

William, a consultant for a major international consulting firm, regularly works with clients in the Middle East. He enjoys working on energy projects and the region offers some of the most exciting opportunities for him. He is open with everyone in his own office, but not with clients in the region. He deflects conversation about his personal life by asking questions about their culture and customs, which he knows they will be interested in sharing. 'When they ask if I'm married, they're trying to be nice and it's not like they are putting me on the spot,' he says. 'It doesn't make me feel awkward. But in a conservative Muslim country, I don't want the baggage of being out. It just wouldn't be helpful.'[33]

Some senior executives believe it is essential to be authentic, even in challenging circumstances. Shielded by their seniority, they can help effect change in their environment.

In the mid-1990s Ivan Scalfarotto moved to Moscow to become the head of human resources for Citibank in Russia, Ukraine and Kazakhstan. Shortly after his arrival, the public affairs office wanted to publish an interview with him in the company newsletter. They asked him a series of questions and, after ten days, his deputy in the department knocked on his door. She came to tell him that the public affairs office was not comfortable that, when asked to describe his family, he said he had 'a partner and a cat'.

Scalfarotto remembers that it was explained to him like this: 'In the Russian translation, "I have a partner" just doesn't sound right. They would suggest that you answer, "I'm not married and I have a cat."' He refused to budge. 'I said, "I don't want to tell people what I'm not. I want to tell people what I am. I want to say that I'm here with someone. I don't care if in Russian it sounds right or not, so please keep the answer."'[34]

A few days later, he received an email from a closeted employee thanking him for the candid interview. 'I'm very proud to have an HR person like you,' the email read. 'I think you're very brave. Please don't tell anyone that I wrote to you.'

THE FUTURE

GENERATIONAL CHANGE IS solving much of the problem of LGBT inclusion. Opponents of gay rights are literally dying out. More and more young people are coming out, and at earlier ages, and that encourages their peers to do the same. They are stepping into the business world with a confidence unknown to previous generations. That confidence is not uniformly strong, as I found during interviews with many of those who are openly gay but still wished to remain anonymous so as to avoid offending their employer or jeopardising their career progression. However, I remain optimistic that we are going in the right direction. Change is on its way. As it can take twenty-five years or longer to get to the position of chief executive in a public company, it is only a matter of time before the openly gay employees of today can become the role model chief executives of tomorrow.

But progress cannot be left to time alone. In my experience, the practical steps set out in this chapter are the right place to start, but they are not sufficient. Policies, resource groups and allies programmes are examples of the changes that businesses must implement.

Companies require leaders who can breathe life into those actions. They require leaders who have a deep understanding of authenticity, and for the emotional and human investment that is required for LGBT employees to feel comfortable coming out at work. As the corporate world gains a new generation of leaders, that understanding is becoming more commonplace. But as the stories in the book have demonstrated, change requires constant attention.

CHAPTER NINE

BEYOND THE CLOSET

I FELT TRAPPED for much of my adult life and was unable to reveal who I was to the world. I led a double life of deep secrecy, and of deep isolation, walled off from those closest to me. It began in school at a time when homosexuality was illegal in the UK. It continued as I entered the sometimes homophobic environment of industry. I had led the transformation of BP from a medium-sized company into the third-largest company in the world. Being gay did not harm my career. But hiding my sexuality made me very unhappy. I kept up the charade until the very end. I was imprisoned by the dread of exposure. I recently talked about this on BBC radio and one of the listeners in his late sixties wrote to me, describing us as members of a 'lost generation'.[1]

My anxiety persisted even as change was unfolding around me. During my final six years at BP, I could see the climate for LGBT people in Britain improving in all important aspects: legally, socially and politically. In 2000, the UK military lifted its ban on openly gay members of the armed forces. Lifting the ban did not result in the large-scale resignations that critics had predicted.[2] The following year, the UK government lowered the age of consent for homosexuals to bring it in line with the law for heterosexuals. In the summer of 2002, Alan Duncan became the first serving Conservative Member of Parliament to come out publicly. 'Living in disguise as a politician in the modern world simply isn't an option,' he said.

'The Tory view has always been "We don't mind, but don't say." Well, that doesn't work any more.'[3]

BP joined the trend and positioned itself to become a symbol of progress. In the summer of 2002, I announced that the company would, for the first time, specifically target minorities, including gay men and lesbians, in its recruitment programme, and that it would offer equal benefits for partners in same-sex relationships.[4] In October, *The Sunday Times* of London interpreted the announcement as a sign that 'change in the City is gathering pace'.[5] Change had been afoot within BP for years. I was championing it but remained careful not to be seen as gay. I had a gnawing feeling that I was doing something wrong every time I made LGBT announcements dispassionately and impersonally. I made them with conviction but without personal emotion.

Progress does not carry everyone with it. As chief executive, I felt that I could not follow the lead of politicians, public figures or even employees within BP who were coming out. I did not want to mire BP in any scandal, nor did I want to undermine the company's standing in conservative countries, where we were responsible for providing employment for tens of thousands of people. Not all of my concerns were related to business. On a personal level, I did not want to reveal that I had been living a lie for so long to close friends, let alone colleagues.

I am certain it is still difficult for some people to understand my reluctance to come out in the light of society's increasing acceptance of LGBT people. In the days after my resignation, the journalist Matthew Parris wrote an eloquent editorial that gave context to my fears. He placed me in a generation of closeted people who could see progress but could not benefit fully from it.

'Men like John Browne have had the misfortune to rise to power and prominence during a time of transition,' he wrote.

'Their careers straddle two eras. When he was a young man, just starting, there is no way he would have made it to the top as an openly gay junior executive. The choice was between celibacy and a discretion bordering on deception. As the years rolled on and attitudes began to shift, it was too late for him to shift with them, disavowing impressions he had allowed to arise at the start. Now he was too exposed.'[6]

Looking back, it is clear that most of my fears were unfounded. I now realise that people understand the pressures that gay men and women face, and can therefore be remarkably forgiving of those who have fenced off a portion of their life. I underestimated the capacity of my friends and colleagues to accept all of me. Much of the problem was inside my head, not inside theirs. When I was forced to acknowledge my sexuality, there were many painful moments, but ultimately my world carried on. I also underestimated the extent to which people already knew, or suspected, that I was gay. No matter how skilled you think you are at hiding your true self, those closest to you, as well as perceptive strangers, will see you through the closet door. Many are quietly hoping that you will step out before you are pulled out by others.

Had I known then what I know now, I would have come out sooner. My eventual departure from BP would have been a much smoother transition and, above all, a more dignified affair. I could have set an encouraging and persuasive example for gay men and women both at BP and in the business world in general. There is one crucial part of my story that would not have changed. And it is exactly this part of my story that I would like others to experience themselves. Parris predicted this in his editorial: 'For all the misery Lord Browne will be enduring over the next few weeks, there will come a morning before the year is out when he awakes with a sudden sense that a Damoclean sword that has hung over him for so long has vanished. His torment this morning will not be entirely unmixed with relief.'[7]

LIBERATION

SINCE MY OUTING in 2007, progress has further accelerated. Many societies are increasingly embracing diversity and LGBT people. Friends and family frequently applaud them for coming out. There are still those who find it difficult to accept the LGBT community, but they tend to be of my generation or older. Their children and grandchildren are significantly less likely to share their views, and they are far more likely to know a gay person, or to have encountered positive portrayals of gay people in popular culture. A majority of people in the US and UK now support equality for gay men and women, including marriage rights and workplace protections. On the global stage, gay rights are increasingly seen as human rights. Respecting them has become a benchmark not just of a tolerant society but also of a civilised one. Societies that accept LGBT people share a common morality, which ultimately strengthens the ties between nations. Those that do not are seen as backward. They will be left behind.

That support has filtered through to the world of business. I am convinced that supportive policies, LGBT resource groups and other initiatives that signal inclusion are necessary to foster an environment in which people feel safe to come out. The elimination of workplace discrimination and giving people the confidence to come out requires everyone involved in business to be constantly vigilant. There are corporations that lead and corporations that lag. The distance between the two can be measured through the quality of the thinking and actions of leadership. Good corporate leaders help instil self-belief in people and empower them to be themselves. Openly gay senior management have a significant opportunity to demonstrate that being out does not limit one's chances for success. At BP, I did not have an openly gay role model, nor did I have the advantage of looking to another chief executive for precedent. Without a gay role model, I failed to be one for others.

Leadership is an essential part of the solution. However, the ultimate responsibility for change rests with LGBT employees themselves. The more people who come out and perform well, the easier it will be for those around them to do the same. A leader can encourage an employee to be confident, but only the employee can use that confidence to come out.

Sally Susman, the communications executive at Pfizer, remembers that she had to choose between denying the existence of her spouse of twenty-five years or being authentic. 'I wear a ring on my ring finger and one time I was in a job interview and the interviewer asked, "What does your husband do?"' she says. 'He was an older gentleman and meant no harm. I had to decide in that moment who I was going to be. I tried to be as polite and gracious as possible. I told him I was lucky enough to have a wonderful partner and she had been supportive of my career, and I hoped that one day he could meet her. In the end I got that job. And I think I got it because he trusted me.'[8]

Much of the problem will be solved in the coming decades as new generations rise to influential positions. They are learning from the example of today's openly gay executives. However, we have reason to be impatient. While researching this book, I was saddened by the anxiety experienced by closeted employees, many of whom are in their late twenties. Their generation enjoys more freedom and openness than any generation before it. Yet, owing to a variety of personal circumstances and experiences, these young men and women are paralysed with fear. Some interviewees did not want to communicate via email because it might leave a trail. Others refused to meet in public spaces because they did not want to risk being seen with a gay person. All their fears strengthened my belief that in thirty years' time there will still be people reluctant to come out. My expectation, though, is that they will be extreme outliers rather than the norm.

For those who do come out, it is important to remember that prejudice exists and will continue against many groups. It exists against women, ethnic minorities and people with disabilities. It exists against short people, old people and overweight people. Gay people are no different.

Remaining attentive to discrimination is important, but so too is recognising that people occasionally make insensitive comments. People tell tasteless jokes. People assume that everyone they deal with is heterosexual. But these instances matter far less than consistent harassment. People must have the confidence to separate poorly judged actions from malicious ones.

Closeted people cannot fully grasp how much their secret weighs them down. In spite of the duplicity and mental energy that being in the closet requires, some people believe this is a sustainable and healthy way to lead their lives.

But living a lie is too costly. One's life should not be built around pleasing the minority of people who may find your sexual orientation objectionable. It should be built around creating meaningful relationships with people who value you for who you are, not what you pretend to be. Kowtowing to those who disapprove of your sexuality suggests that their comfort is more important than your own. It is not. People often do not account for what Peter Sands, of Standard Chartered, aptly refers to as the 'hidden costs of hidden lives'.[9]

We all want to make a contribution. Working life provides one of the most obvious routes to fulfil that desire. Coming out allowed me to fuse my personal and professional worlds. Although I am no longer a chief executive, I have maintained a high level of productivity. In some ways, I am sure that I am more productive. I no longer waste time trying to hide things away.

The freedom that so many LGBT people now enjoy is based on centuries of sacrifice and success. Enlightenment thinkers questioned why leaders criminalised sexual identity. Some psychologists fought to define homosexuality as a normal part of life rather than a mental illness. Activists, artists and politicians spoke out, even when faced with the risk of humiliation and violence. David Hockney treated homosexuality expressly in his paintings, and James Baldwin bravely shared the isolation of being gay in a heterosexual world. Drag queens at the Stonewall Inn said they would not accept oppression any longer, and defied policemen who carried clubs and guns. Harvey Milk campaigned for gay rights in San Francisco, and was murdered. Each of these people has honoured the memory of the LGBT people who came before them, usually in a world that was harsher and less accepting of difference. From the gay men burned at the stake during the Middle Ages to those eliminated by the Nazis and to the LGBT men and women living in oppression in parts of the world today, progress is never even or permanent.

In the year I have spent writing this book, I have learned much about these great sacrifices that people have made in the name of authenticity. Thanks to them, we are now better and act with greater confidence than ever before. I have learned a lot about the contributions that companies, their leaders, and their employees are making today to foster better working environments. In doing so, they are also creating a healthier society, and taking important steps to ensure that the lessons of the past are learned – hopefully for the last time. Their efforts, combined with broader shifts in attitude, have created unprecedented momentum in large parts of the world. It should be evident from the stories in this book that the challenges to LGBT people are diminishing. But constant vigilance is needed to prevent reversion to the darkest part of history. The history of minority persecution is one of recurring tragedies.

Those of us with the opportunity to live freely should seize it. Business has done much to create a great vision of that opportunity, but it can only come to life if LGBT people and their supporters are willing to nurture it. Gay people should not sacrifice their own happiness to appease someone with antiquated beliefs. It is not selfish to put yourself first. You will do more to better the world when you can be authentic.

I do not approach this conclusion lightly. I have listened to the warnings of history. I have listened to the concerns of people, young and old, about why coming out may impact on their careers in their specific circumstances. The key word here is 'may'.

Coming out can be terrifying in the moment. But as someone who came out in a very public way, I can tell you that doing so will force you to be honest, transparent and brave. In the end, those qualities will serve you well, no matter how high you have already climbed or how far you still have to go. More often than not, the risk will be worth the reward.

Taking that one step will shatter the glass and reveal the true beauty of life. You will think bigger, aim higher and be twice the person you were in the closet.

ACKNOWLEDGEMENTS

I HAVE BEEN finishing this book in the wide open spaces of Patagonia, Chile. The volcanoes, mountains, rivers and the unpopulated rainforest vividly remind me of the insignificance of human beings. In the broad scales of geography and history, nothing is of consequence. However, in our own time and context, there is much of meaning that affects our lives. It is my hope that this book, which reflects a moment in time in 2013, will make a contribution to those who feel alone, different, hurt or confused because they are gay, lesbian, bisexual or transgender. I hope too that it will encourage the majority, who are straight, to welcome, include and respect the LGBT population.

Many people have helped make this book possible. A large number of them agreed to be interviewed and gave generously of their time. I am grateful to them all. They are listed immediately following these acknowledgements. I am also indebted to all those who agreed to be interviewed for this book but who wished to remain anonymous. I hope that they will one day consider telling the world who they are.

Gail Rebuck first approached me with the suggestion that I write something about being gay in business; she is the 'godmother' of this book and I am most grateful to her for giving me the confidence to write it.

My agent Ed Victor has provided his usual wise advice from the inception of this book to its publication. Ed Faulkner, my publisher at Random House UK, and Jonathan

Burnham and Hollis Heimbouch, the publishing team at HarperCollins USA, have provided invaluable guidance. I thank all of them for the comments, suggestions and wisdom they have provided over the past eighteen months.

I am fortunate to have friends and colleagues who have given generously of their time to review critically early drafts of this book. I owe enormous thanks to Brian Masters, distinguished author and winner of the Crime Writers' Association Gold Dagger; Kate Bucknell, novelist and editor of Christopher Isherwood's diaries; Emran Mian, formerly a director in the UK Civil Service who looked after me brilliantly while I led a review of higher education and then when I was the UK government's lead independent director, also a novelist and now director of the Social Market Foundation; Ben Moxham, formerly a colleague at BP and then at Riverstone; David Yelland, a close and valued advisor; Mark Hutchinson, my publicist in the UK; Peter Sands, chief executive officer of Standard Chartered plc; Dev Sanyal, a senior executive at BP; Gini Savage, a close friend who introduced me to Ruan Bone and *Lunch* magazine forty years too late; Rod Christie-Miller, a great lawyer who has been involved with my story since early 2007; and Ben Richards, a highly promising young sociologist who reviewed the quantitative studies cited in this book with great care and attention.

Matthew Powell, my chief of staff, has added to his considerable workload to do a variety of editing tasks. Tommy Stadlen, my project director, has also contributed his expertise to difficult passages. My executive assistant, Sarah Paynter, who has been with me for many years, gave her own account of my final days at BP and helped me refresh my memory of the tsunami of inspiring letters of support from 2007, all of which she had preserved. I thank them all for doing far more than I ever asked of them.

William Lee Adams spent over a year of his life working with me on this book. He is a remarkable professional journalist, researcher and writer with considerable knowledge of LGBT matters. I thank him for all he has done, with such good grace and humour, for this book. Without him *The Glass Closet* would never have been written.

I want to thank my partner, Nghi Nguyen, for his support not only in general but also specifically for working on the final edits while we were travelling in Uruguay and Chile. He made getting to the final manuscript worthwhile.

Finally, I want to acknowledge all those people, particularly those who were gay, who developed my life in good ways and bad. They are the foundation of this book.

John Browne
London and Patagonia
January 2014

BIOGRAPHIES

CHARLES ALLEN is the chairman of Global Radio Group and 2 Sisters Food Group, and the former chief executive of ITV, Granada Group and Compass Group. A life peer in the House of Lords, he sat on the board of the London Organising Committee of the Olympic and Paralympic Games.

M. V. LEE BADGETT is the director of the Center for Public Policy and Administration at the University of Massachusetts Amherst, and a senior scholar at The Williams Institute at the University of California, Los Angeles. She is the author of *When Gay People Get Married: What Happens When Societies Legalize Same-Sex Marriage.*

TEDDY BASHAM-WITHERINGTON is the chief marketing officer of Out & Equal Workplace Advocates, and the former co-president of InterPride, the international association of gay pride coordinators.

ANTONIA BELCHER is a founding partner of MHBC, an independent building consultancy in London. She also serves on the board of directors for the Chartered Surveyors Training Trust, which provides surveying apprenticeships for young people, regardless of their academic, social or financial circumstances.

PATTI BELLINGER is executive director and adjunct lecturer at the Center for Public Leadership at the Harvard Kennedy School, and the former executive director of executive education at Harvard Business School. She previously served as group vice president of global diversity and inclusion at BP in London.

SELISSE BERRY is the founder and chief executive officer of Out & Equal Workplace Advocates, the world's largest non-profit organisation specifically dedicated to creating safe and equitable workplaces for lesbian, gay, bisexual and transgender people. She is the editor of *Out & Equal at Work*, and has master's degrees in education and theology from the University of Texas and San Francisco Theological Seminary respectively.

MICHAEL BISHOP is the former owner of the airline BMI and the former chairman of Channel 4. A life peer in the House of Lords, he was one of the first prominent British businessmen to come out publicly.

GUY BLACK is the executive director of the Telegraph Media Group, the news publisher of *The Daily Telegraph* and *The Sunday Telegraph*. He is also a life peer in the House of Lords.

JOHN BOSCO is a mental health support worker and book-keeper in Southampton. In 2001, he fled his native Uganda for the UK after a police crackdown on the gay community.

CLAUDIA BRIND-WOODY is the vice president and managing director for intellectual property licensing at IBM, and the co-chair of IBM's Executive Task Force for LGBT Diversity. She has also served on the board of directors for Lambda Legal and the board of advisors for John C. Stennis Institute of Government.

BETH BROOKE is the global vice chair for public policy at EY, and a member of the firm's global executive board. *Forbes* magazine has named her one of the world's 100 most powerful women six times.

RENEE D. BROWN is a senior vice president and director of social media for Wells Fargo in Charlotte, North Carolina. An out lesbian mother, she also serves on the board of Out & Equal Workplace Advocates.

CAROLE CAMERON is a mechanical engineering senior manager for Lockheed Martin and is responsible for an array of space-craft and rocket component design. She is on the board of the LGBT Pride employee group and has represented the company at a number of national diversity events.

MICHAEL CASHMAN is a Labour Member of the European Parliament for the West Midlands in the UK, and previously served on the Labour Party's National Executive Committee between 1998 and 2012. A distinguished actor and singer, he is perhaps best known for his role as Colin Russell in the BBC soap opera *EastEnders*.

JUSTIN CHENETTE is the youngest openly gay legislator in the US, having won election to the Maine House of Representatives at the age of twenty-one. He serves as the vice chair of the Youth Caucus, is a state director for the Young Elected Officials Network and is the founder and president of the Saco Bay Center for Civic Engagement.

DARREN COOPER is a senior consultant for Out Now, a leading specialist LGBT consulting firm. He has helped drive ground-breaking diversity projects, research studies and communications initiatives aimed at LGBT people for leading organisations such as visitBerlin, Lloyds Banking Group and Barclaycard.

JONATHAN COOPER is chief executive of the London-based Human Dignity Trust, a human rights organisation that works to de-criminalise homosexuality around the world. A practising barrister in the UK, he has worked with the Foreign & Commonwealth Office, the Ministry of Justice, the Home Office and the Director of Service Prosecutions.

CHRIS CRESPO is a director in the Americas Inclusiveness Center of Excellence at EY and a co-founder of the firm's LGBTA affinity group Beyond. She leads EY's efforts with inclusiveness and flexibility throughout the US and Canada with a focus on professional networks and LGBTA inclusiveness strategy.

MIRANDA CURTIS is the chairman of Waterstones and a non-executive director of Marks & Spencer and Liberty Global Inc. During her twenty-year career with Liberty, she has negotiated and managed joint ventures across Europe and Asia Pacific, most notably Japan.

DEBORAH DAGIT served as a chief diversity officer at three different Fortune 200 companies over a period of twenty-two years, and is currently president of a diversity and inclusion consulting practice, debdagitdiversity.com. As a lifelong LGBT ally and a person with a visible disability, she is often asked to speak about her unique personal and professional journey.

JEFF DAVIS is a managing director and global head of capital markets for Barclays in London. He has also served as an operating executive and division president of Dow Jones & Company, and as executive vice president at CBS MarketWatch.

RALPH DE CHABERT is the chief diversity officer at Brown-Forman in Louisville, Kentucky. He previously led diversity and inclusion efforts at McKesson Corporation, and was chief diversity officer at Safeway.

MARIA DE LA O is a San Francisco-based journalist who has covered LGBT and other issues for more than twenty years. She currently blogs for the 'She the People' section of *The Washington Post* and is producing a feature documentary about women starting a band in the West Bank.

DENIS DISON is the senior vice president for programmes at the Gay & Lesbian Victory Fund and Institute in Washington DC. He manages a team delivering training and executive development programming for openly LGBT public leaders.

JUSTIN DONAHUE is a principal consultant for enterprise software implementations at the Silicon Valley office of Oracle. He is a graduate of Lockheed Martin's Leadership Development Program and is the past chair of Lockheed Martin's Space Systems Company's Pride organisation.

JACK DRESCHER, MD, is a psychiatrist and psychoanalyst in private practice in New York City. He is past president of the Group for Advancement of Psychiatry, a distinguished fellow of the American Psychiatric Association and a past chair of APA's Committee on GLB Issues.

TODD EVANS is the president and CEO of Rivendell Media, the LGBT media rep firm that represents most LGBT publications for national advertising in the US and Canada. Todd is also publisher of *Press Pass Q*, the industry newsletter for LGBT media professionals.

CHRIS FARMER is head of communications for Bain & Company and a member of BGLAD, the organisation's GLB group. He is a former president of the Oxford Union.

GARY FEIERTAG is a strategy and performance manager at BP, and a chartered accountant. He is a past chair of BP's UK LGBT employee network and continues to be a champion for LGBT equality in the workplace.

MIKE FELDMAN is president of the Large Enterprise Operation at the Xerox Corporation and serves on the Board of Directors at Out & Equal Workplace Advocates. Prior to joining Xerox, he spent twenty-four years at Hewlett-Packard.

FRANÇOIS FEUILLAT is a partner at the London office of international law firm Vinson & Elkins. An expert on complex cross-border mergers and acquisitions, he has advised on energy deals totalling more than $100 billion.

DEENA FIDAS is the director of the Workplace Project at the Human Rights Campaign in Washington DC. She previously worked in fund-raising for the American Civil Liberties Union and Hillary Clinton for President.

JEFF FRANK is a professor of economics at Royal Holloway and Bedford New College, University of London, where he was the founding head of department. He has taught finance as a visiting professor at Harvard University and the University of California, Berkeley.

ADRIAN FULFORD is a judge on the Court of Appeal of England and Wales. He was one of the first eighteen judges sworn into the International Criminal Court at The Hague, on which he served from 2003 to 2012.

THOMAS GENSEMER is US chief strategy officer at global public relations and communications firm Burson-Marsteller. Previously, he was a co-founder, managing partner and chief executive of digital public affairs firm Blue State Digital.

AIDAN DENIS GILLIGAN is founder and CEO of SciCom – Making Sense of Science, an international consulting practice specialising in complex science communication for governmental and non-governmental groups. He has held various senior communications roles at the College of Europe and the European Commission, and sits on the governing board of Euroscience.

ALLAN GILMOUR is the former vice chairman of Ford Motor Company and the president emeritus of Wayne State University. He has served on the boards of corporations including Dow Chemical, Prudential Financial and Whirlpool.

VANDY BETH GLENN is a freelance writer and editor based in Decatur, Georgia. She was the plaintiff in the landmark civil rights case, Glenn v. Brumby.

STEPHEN GOLDEN is the Asia Pacific head of global leadership and diversity at Goldman Sachs. He and his civil partner, Richard, live in Hong Kong.

ANNA GRODZKA is the first openly transgender Member of Parliament in Poland and an active member of the Parliamentary Women's Group. She has also served as president of the Alma Press and as a senior cadet sergeant in the Polish military.

KAPIL GUPTA is a researcher at the Human Dignity Trust in London. He completed his MA in Human Rights Practice under the Erasmus Mundus scholarship of the European Commission and holds a bachelor's degree in law from the National Law Institute University, Bhopal (India).

SIRI HARRISON is an internationally recognised clinical psychologist, specialising in affirmative psychotherapy with the LGBT community. She currently practises in central London and regularly contributes to the media, educating the public on LGBT health-related issues.

APRIL HAWKINS is a communications manager at Out & Equal Workplace Advocates. She has a master's degree in Middle Eastern studies from the University of Tel Aviv, and currently sits on the board of directors for the NorCal National Lesbian and Gay Journalists Association. She previously worked with the United Nations High Commissioner for Refugees in Tel Aviv, Israel.

CAZ HILDEBRAND is a founding partner of Here Design, a London-based design studio that has worked with clients including Thames & Hudson and the Victoria & Albert Museum. She is also the co-author of the graphic cookbook *The Geometry of Pasta*.

THOMAS HITZLSPERGER is a retired football player who has played for some of Europe's top clubs, including Aston Villa, West Ham and Stuttgart, and the German national team. In January 2014, he became the first Premier League player ever to come out.

JULIA HOGGETT is a managing director at Bank of America Merrill Lynch, responsible for short-term fixed income origination, covered bonds, financial institution flow financing and green debt capital markets for the Europe, Middle East and Africa (EMEA) region. She also acts as co-chair of the firm's LGBT EMEA network and has a long history of working to help advance diversity and inclusion policies within the financial services sector.

JEFF HOLLAND is a co-founder of Liongate Capital Management, a hedge fund firm with $7 billion in assets under management and advisory. *Institutional Investor* named him a 'Rising Star of Hedge Funds' and *Financial News* cited him among the '40 Under 40' in hedge funds.

IAN JOHNSON is the CEO of LGBT consulting firm Out Now. He has been described as a 'global LGBT thought leader' and has advised governments, NGOs and many of the world's leading companies on how to understand and meet the needs of LGBT people.

TOM JOHNSON is corporate controller and chief accounting officer at The Clorox Company in Oakland, California. He was a founding member of the company's LGBT employee resource group Clorox Pride, and also serves as president of the board of directors for Out & Equal Workplace Advocates.

BINNA KANDOLA is a senior partner and co-founder of Pearn Kandola, a business psychology consultancy in London. He is the author of several books including *The Value of Difference: Eliminating Bias in Organisations*.

ERIKA KARP is the founder and CEO of consulting firm Cornerstone Capital, Inc., which applies the principles of sustainable finance and economics to facilitate the flow of capital globally. She is the former head of global sector research at UBS Investment Bank, and is a founding board member of the Sustainability Accounting Standards Board.

BILLIE JEAN KING is a former world number one tennis player and the winner of thirty-nine Grand Slam singles, doubles and mixed doubles titles. She was awarded the 2009 Presidential Medal of Freedom for her work advocating for the rights of women and the LGBT community.

DAMIAN LEESON is public policy director at Tesco. He has also served as managing director of public policy at the FTI consulting and as director of group public affairs at Prudential PLC.

ANNA MANN is a co-founder of MWM, a leading international executive search and board advisory consulting firm. She has acted as a specialist advisor to many of the world's leading corporations on board performance, capability and succession.

IVAN MASSOW is an entrepreneur and the former chairman of London's Institute of Contemporary Arts. In 1990, he established the first financial advisory firm in Britain aimed at gay clients, many of whom faced higher mortgage and insurance premiums because of their sexuality.

BRIAN MCNAUGHT has, since 1974, been a popular educator on lesbian, gay, bisexual and transgender issues, and has spoken globally to corporate leaders on related workplace issues. Named 'the godfather of gay diversity and sensitivity training' by *The New York Times*, he is the author of six books and features in seven educational DVDs.

WILLIAM J. MORAN, JR. is a senior vice president with Merrill Lynch in Washington DC. He also leads the firm's nationwide LGBT financial services team and sits on its diversity and inclusion council and on the boards of numerous LGBT non-profit organisations.

PETER MURRAY is a public affairs professional based in London. He is head of government affairs at Arup, an independent firm of designers, planners, engineers and consultants.

MARTINA NAVRATILOVA is a former world number one tennis player and the winner of fifty-nine Grand Slam singles, doubles and mixed doubles titles. She currently sits on the advisory board of Athlete Ally, a non-profit organisation focused on ending homophobia and transphobia in sports.

BOB PAGE is the founder and CEO of Replacements Ltd., the world's largest retailer of old and new china, crystal, silver and collectibles. Recognised nationally as a leader in the fight for LGBT equality, he lives in North Carolina with his partner of twenty-five years, Dale Frederiksen, and twin sons, Ryan and Owen.

TREVOR PHILLIPS is the deputy chair of the steering committee of the National Equality Standard in London, and a director of the New York-based Center for Talent Innovation. He is the former chairman of the UK's Equality and Human Rights Commission and the author of *Windrush: The Irresistible Rise of Multi-Racial Britain*.

MARTIN POPPLEWELL runs the London-based media consultancy Coconut Communications. He joined the BBC as a graduate trainee and went on to present on the BBC News Channel and Sky News.

LANCE PRICE is the founder and executive director of the Kaleidoscope Trust, a London-based charity that campaigns to uphold the human rights of LGBT people around the world. He was a special advisor to Prime Minister Tony Blair and is a former director of communications for the Labour Party.

PAUL REED is the CEO of BP's Integrated Supply and Trading business responsible for the sale of oil and gas production, refinery feedstock, the marketing of fuels supply and all trading activity within the BP Group. He is the executive sponsor of BP's LGBT network.

MARGARET REGAN is the president and CEO of the FutureWork Institute, a global consulting firm that addresses workplace issues including diversity and inclusion. She has consulted with many large global corporations, researching and addressing issues in North America, Europe, Latin America, Asia and Africa.

RACHEL RISKIND is an assistant professor of psychology at Guilford College, North Carolina. She conducts research on sexual orientation, reproductive health and bias, and over the past several years has curated and analysed data from the sexuality Implicit Association Test (IAT).

IVAN SCALFAROTTO is a member of Italy's parliament and the former vice president of the Democratic Party. In 2010, he founded Parks – Liberi e Uguali, a non-profit organisation that helps companies in Italy implement equal opportunity policies for LGBT employees.

TODD SEARS is the founder and principal of Coda Leadership, a strategic advising firm that helps companies align their diversity and inclusion efforts with their business objectives. He is also the founder of Out Leadership, which organises the Out on the

Street LGBT leadership summits for the financial services industry in New York, London and Hong Kong.

DAVID SHELLEY is the group publisher at Little, Brown in London. He has edited and published authors including Mitch Albom, Mark Billingham, J. K. Rowling and Val McDermid.

ANTONIO SIMOES is the head of HSBC in the UK and was previously a partner at McKinsey & Co. and an associate at Goldman Sachs. He was appointed a Young Global Leader of the World Economic Forum in 2009 and came first in the 2013 ranking of LGBT business leaders by OUTstanding in Business.

CHRIS SMITH is the Chairman of the UK Environment Agency and a life peer in the House of Lords. In 1984, he became the country's first openly gay Member of Parliament and served as the Secretary of State for Culture, Media and Sport.

KIRK SNYDER is an assistant professor at the Marshall School of Business at the University of Southern California. Recognised as an expert on business diversity issues and inclusive leadership, he is the author of *The G Quotient* and *Lavender Road to Success*.

MARTIN SORRELL has been the group chief executive of multinational advertising and public relations firm WPP since 1986. He is also non-executive director of Formula One and Aloca Inc.

MARGARET S. STUMPP is senior advisor to Quantitative Management Associates (QMA), where she previously served as chief investment officer for over two decades. She is involved in quantitative research in asset allocation, security selection and portfolio construction, and holds a PhD in economics from Brown University.

KAREN SUMBERG currently works in diversity at Google. She was with the Center for Talent Innovation for eight years, leading research including 'The Power of Out' and 'The Power of Out 2.0'.

BEN SUMMERSKILL is chief executive of Stonewall, the London-based lesbian, gay and bisexual equality organisation. He is a former commissioner on Britain's Equality and Human Rights Commission.

SALLY SUSMAN is executive vice president of corporate affairs for Pfizer, one of the world's premier biopharmaceutical companies. She serves on the boards of the Library of Congress Trust Fund, WPP, the International Rescue Committee and the US India Business Council.

MIKE SYERS is a partner at EY and is responsible for the New York Transaction Advisory Services real estate and hospitality industry practice. He is a founding member of EY's LGBTA employee group, and is a member of the firm's Inclusiveness Advisory Council of Partners.

ROSALYN TAYLOR O'NEALE is a principal consultant at diversity consulting firm Cook Ross and the author of *Seven Keys to Success: Unlocking the Passion for Diversity*. She served as vice president and chief diversity and inclusion officer at the Campbell Soup Company from 2008 to 2012.

BROOK WARD is a gas settlements manager within BP's North America gas and power business unit in Houston. He has been an active member in BP's business resource group, BP Pride, since its inception and is currently one of the national leads for the group in the US.

STEVEN WARDLAW is partner-in-charge at the London office of international law firm Baker Botts. He was previously partner-in-charge of the Moscow office, and has significant experience advising energy companies, regulatory bodies and governments on projects undertaken in the energy sector in Asia, Europe and the Middle East.

RICK WELTS is the president and chief operating officer of the Golden State Warriors basketball team. He has also served as president and chief executive officer of the Phoenix Suns, and as executive vice president, chief marketing officer and president of NBA Properties.

BOBBY WILKINSON is an assistant vice president within the member experience group at USAA Insurance and Financial Services in San Antonio, Texas. He sits on the boards of Out & Equal Workplace Advocates and the San Antonio Pride Center.

GAVIN WILLS is head of corporate services and real estate for Goldman Sachs in EMEA. Based in London, he is also co-head of the firm's LGBT network in the region.

DANIEL WINTERFELDT is head of international capital markets and diversity and inclusion partner at the London office of CMS Cameron McKenna. He is also the founder and co-chair of the InterLaw Diversity Forum for LGBT Networks and was named 'Legal Innovator of the Year' by the *Financial Times* in 2012.

BOB WITECK is president and founder of US-based Witeck Communications and author of *Business Inside Out*. He is a communications strategist, an entrepreneur and a pioneer in LGBT demographics, market research and media relations.

CHUCK WOLFE is the president and CEO of the Gay & Lesbian Victory Fund and Institute. He also serves on the board of trustees at his alma mater, Stetson University, Florida.

KLAUS WOWEREIT is the governing mayor of Berlin. He has also served as president of the Bundesrat and vice chairman of the Social Democratic Party.

LOUISE YOUNG spent most of her career as a software engineer at the Dallas offices of Texas Instruments and Raytheon. She is better known as a pioneering lesbian activist, especially in the area of workplace equality.

ENDNOTES

A NOTE ON STATISTICS

THIS BOOK REFERS to a number of statistics produced by a variety of different types of study. Care has been taken to investigate the sources of each of the statistics, including the methods used by each study, together with their suitability for making the kinds of claims each statistic has been used for in this book. Each source, along with its methods, was critically assessed. However, some general comments and qualifications on the reliability of the statistics used are necessary. With each of the studies cited, there are two broad sources of potential error: one relating to the sampling methods used; and the other relating to non-sampling response errors, particularly those arising from the fact that questions on sexual orientation and identity may be considered sensitive.

With regards to potential errors created by the sampling methods used, there are, generally speaking, three different types of study cited in this book. The first type uses data from nationally representative surveys based on probability sampling, and is the most reliable type of study for generating reasonably reliable statistics about a (often national) population. The second type uses data from surveys that do not use probability sampling, which means that some units in the population could be more likely to be selected than others. These studies instead use weights to attempt to make the data, to some extent, representative of a general population. This method of sampling is not as reliable as the methods used in the first type, so the data from these studies should be treated with more caution. These methods are sometimes necessary, though, to capture information on minority groups like the LGBT group, because relevant questions are often not available in surveys using full probability samples, and because this second type of survey can be conducted more easily and cheaply. The third type of study may feature more in-depth interviewing procedures, but does not attempt to make data representative of a general population at all. Surveys using these methods can yield interesting insights into the experiences described by the people surveyed, but statistics based on them should not necessarily be taken to imply anything about a population wider than the specific group of people surveyed.

Where studies were available, this book uses the first type of study when citing statistics comparing differences between groups in a general population (often a national population such as that of the US or UK). However, questions on sexual identity and orientation, and on the experiences of LGBT people at work, are unfortunately not included in many large-scale probability-based national surveys. Where this is the case, statistics are cited from studies of the second type, although the results should be treated with more caution. Studies of the third type are used in this book to highlight the life stories, experiences and motivations of particular people. Data on transgender people in particular can be very hard to gather, so this third type of study is particularly important for understanding the experiences of some groups of people. Nevertheless, where these studies are cited, it is important to note that their results are not representative, for example, of all transgender people in the US. Where studies in this third category have been cited, the reader should note that they may not be representative.

However, sources of error in survey data can also derive from non-sampling response errors. This is particularly likely to be a problem where the questions are especially sensitive, such as those on sexual identity and orientation and their interaction with workplace prejudice and discrimination. The sensitivity of survey questions can come from three different sources. First, a question itself might be seen as potentially intrusive; second, there might be risks attached to answering the question truthfully; and third, the answers given might be influenced by 'social desirability bias'. Intrusiveness refers to the fact that if, within the culture in which a question is asked, it is seen as particularly private or taboo, respondents might simply refuse to answer the question. This non-response issue becomes particularly problematic if there are systematic differences between those answering the question and those refusing to do so. Where risks are involved in truthfully answering a question, there may be a bias towards respondents not revealing such risky information. Examples include questions requesting the reporting of illegal behaviour, such as drug use. By contrast, social desirability bias refers to respondents' tendency to admit to socially desirable traits and behaviours and to deny socially undesirable ones. This bias means that survey respondents might be more likely to report attitudes and behaviour ostensibly considered to be desirable by society, and might be less likely to report attitudes and behaviour considered to be undesirable. Empirical studies have attempted to estimate the magnitude of biases such as these, and have found evidence of substantial under-reporting of same-sex sexual behaviours and bisexual or homosexual identification in survey-style questions. There is also evidence to suggest that homophobic attitudes may be under-reported. These biases can be mitigated to a certain extent by particular features of research design, such as ensuring that a questionnaire is completed without an interviewer being present. It may not be possible, however, to eliminate them entirely, and for this reason the statistics cited in this book should be treated with some caution.

For further information see:

Bryman, A., *Social Research Methods* (Oxford: Oxford University Press, 2012).

Coffman, K.; Coffman, L.; Marzilli Ericson, K., 'The Size of the LGBT Population and the Magnitude of Anti-Gay Sentiment are Substantially Underestimated', National Bureau of Economic Research, NBER Working Paper No. 19508, 2013.

Krumpal, I., 'Determinants of social desirability bias in sensitive surveys: a literature review', *Quality & Quantity*, 2013, 47(4): 2025–2047.

Tourangeau, R. and Yan, T., 'Sensitive Questions in Surveys', *Psychological Bulletin*, 2007, 133(5): 859–883.

PROLOGUE

1   Hewlett, Sylvia Ann; Sears, Todd; Sumberg, Karen; Fargnoli, Christina, 'The Power of Out 2.0: LGBT in the Workplace', Center for Talent Innovation, 2013, p. 1.

2   Ibid., p. 27.

CHAPTER 1: HIDE-AND-SEEK

1   Cowell, Alan, 'BP Chief Resigns Amid Battle With Tabloid', *The New York Times*, 1 May 2007. Accessed via *The New York Times* website: http://www.nytimes.com/2007/05/01/business/worldbusiness/01cnd-oil.html?pagewanted=all&_r=0.

2   Smith, David, 'Four decades of glory ruined by a white lie', *The Guardian*, 6 May 2007. Accessed via *The Guardian* website: http://www.theguardian.com/media/2007/may/06/pressandpublishing.oilandpetrol.

3   Following the Second World War, Italian businessman Enrico Mattei coined the term 'the Seven Sisters' to describe the Anglo-Saxon companies that dominated the global petroleum industry. The group consisted of the Anglo-Persian Oil Company (the forerunner to BP), Gulf Oil (now part of Chevron), Standard Oil of California (now part of Chevron), Texaco (now part of Chevron), Royal Dutch Shell, Standard Oil of New Jersey and Standard Oil Company of New York. The latter two eventually merged to make up ExxonMobil. By the end of the 1960s, these companies controlled 85 per cent of the world's oil reserves.

4   On 5 June 1981, the United States Centers for Disease Control and Prevention (CDC) published the first official report of an unusual condition that was affecting five gay men in Los Angeles. The Associated Press and the *Los Angeles Times* covered the news, leading doctors around the country to contact the CDC with similar cases. By the end of the year, doctors had reported a total of 270 cases in

which gay men demonstrated severe immune deficiency. For more information on the history of HIV/AIDS, consult 'A Timeline of AIDS' on the AIDS.gov website.

5   Levy, Geoffrey, 'Lord Browne: The Sun King who lost his shine', *Daily Mail*, 1 May 2007. Accessed via the *Daily Mail* website: http://www.dailymail.co.uk/news/article-451947/Lord-Browne-The-Sun-King-lost-shine.html.

6   Macalister, Terry, 'A year that went from turbulent to terminal,' *The Guardian*, 2 May 2007. Accessed via *The Guardian* website: www.theguardian.com/media/2007/may/02/pressandpublishing.business1.

7   Cavafy, C. P., *Passions and Ancient Days*, translated by Edmund Keeley and George Savidis (New York: The Dial Press, 1971), p. 31.

CHAPTER 2: BEAUTY AND BIGOTRY

1   Historians and archaeologists are not certain where the cup was discovered. However, reports from the early twentieth century suggest that it was found buried in Bittir, approximately six miles from Jerusalem. See Williams, Dyfri, *The Warren Cup* (London: The British Museum Press, 2006), pp. 47–8.

2   Morrison, Richard, 'The somnolent jeunes of la belle France', 17 January 2003. Accessed via *The Times* (of London) website: http://www.thetimes.co.uk/tto/opinion/columnists/richardmorrison/article2045296.ece.

3   Frost, Stuart, 'The Warren Cup: Secret Museums, Sexuality, and Society' in *Gender, Sexuality and Museums: A Routledge Reader*, edited by Amy K. Levin (New York: Routledge, 2010), p. 144.

4   MacGregor, Neil, *A History of the World in 100 Objects*, Episode 36, Warren Cup. Radio transcript accessed via the BBC website: http://www.bbc.co.uk/ahistoryoftheworld/about/transcripts/episode36/.

5   Marguerite Yourcenar used these words to celebrate the homosexuality of the Greek poet Constantine Cavafy in an essay introducing a collection of his poems. See Yourcenar, Marguerite, *Présentation critique de Constantin Cavafy 1863–1933, suivie d'une traduction des Poèmes par Marguerite Yourcenar et Constantin Dimaras* (Paris: Gallimard, 1978), p. 41; cited in White, Edmund, *The Burning Library: Writings on Art, Politics and Sexuality, 1969–1993* (London: Picador, 1995), pp. 350–1.

6   Aldrich, Robert, 'Homosexuality in Greece and Rome' in *Gay Life and Culture: A World History*, edited by Robert Aldrich (London: Thames & Hudson, 2006), pp. 29–30.

7   Ibid., p. 30.

8   See Plutarch's *Erotikos* (761d); and Dowden, Ken, *The Uses of Greek Mythology* (New York: Routledge, 1992), p. 82.

9   Neill, James, *The Origins and Role of Same-sex Relations in Human Societies* (Jefferson: McFarland & Company, 2009), p. 147.

10 Aldrich, Robert and Wotherspoon, Garry, *Who's Who in Gay and Lesbian History* (London: Routledge, 2001), p. 174.

11 Two excerpts from the Book of Leviticus refer to homosexuality. Leviticus 18:22 states, 'You shall not lie with a man as with a woman: that is an abomination.' According to Leviticus 20:13, 'If a man has intercourse with a man, as with a woman, they both commit an abomination: they shall be put to death; their blood shall be on their own heads.'

12 Ellis, Havelock, *Studies in the Psychology of Sex: Sexual Inversion* (Honolulu: University Press of the Pacific, 2001; reprinted from the 1906 edition), p. 207.

13 Naphy, William, *Born to Be Gay: A History of Homosexuality* (Stroud: Tempus, 2006), p. 100.

14 Ibid.; see also Fone, Byrne, *Homophobia: A History* (New York: Picador USA, 2000), pp. 186–7.

15 Fone, p. 192.

16 Naphy, p. 109; see also Rocke, Michael J., *Forbidden Friendships: Homosexuality and Male Culture in Renaissance Florence* (New York: Oxford University Press, 1996), pp. 20–1.

17 Fone, p. 193.

18 Parkinson, R. B., *A Little Gay History: Desire and Diversity Across the World* (London: The British Museum Press, 2013), p. 74.

19 Corriveau, Patrice, *Judging Homosexuals: A History of Gay Persecution in Quebec and France* (Vancouver: UBC Press, 2011), p. 165.

20 Frank, David John; Boutcher, Steven A.; Camp, Bayliss, 'The Reform of Sodomy Laws from a World Society Perspective' in *Queer Mobilizations: LGBT Activists Confront the Law*, edited by Scott Barclay, Mary Bernstein and Anna-Maria Marshall (New York: New York University Press, 2009), p. 136.

21 Sibalis, Michael, 'The Age of Enlightenment and Revolution' in *Gay Life and Culture: A World History,* edited by Robert Aldrich (London: Thames & Hudson, 2006), p. 123.

22 Ibid.

23 As quoted in Hyde, H. Montgomery, *The Other Love: An Historical and Contemporary Survey of Homosexuality in Britain* (London: Granada Publishing, 1970), p. 138.

24 Human Rights Watch, 'This Alien Legacy: The Origins of "Sodomy" Laws in British Colonialism', 2008. Accessed via the Human Rights Watch website: http://www.hrw.org/sites/default/files/reports/lgbt1208_webwcover.pdf.

25 Kirby, Michael, 'The sodomy offence: England's least lovely criminal law export?' in *Human Rights, Sexual Orientation and Gender Identity in the Commonwealth: Struggles for Decriminalisation and Change*, edited by Corinne Lennox and Matthew Waites (London: Institute of Commonwealth Studies, 2013), p. 67.

26 According to the Human Dignity Trust, forty-four countries that were once colonies, dominions, protectorates or associated states of the British Empire still criminalised homosexuality at the end of 2013. Two additional entities formerly under British rule also criminalised homosexuality. They are the Cook Islands, which now form a self-governing state in free association with New Zealand, and the Turkish Republic of Northern Cyprus, which proclaimed its independence from Cyprus in 1983.

27 Between April 1993 and August 2013, more than 36 million people visited the United States Holocaust Memorial Museum. For more information, visit http://www.ushmm.org/.

28 Langer, Emily, 'Rudolf Brazda dies; gay man who survived Nazi concentration camp was 98', *The Washington Post*, 7 August 2011. Accessed via *The Washington Post* website: http://www.washingtonpost.com/local/obituaries/rudolf-brazda-dies-gay-man-who-survived-nazi-concentration-camp-was-98/2011/08/05/gIQAUlb90I_story.html.

29 Giles, Geoffrey, '"The Most Unkindest Cut of All": Castration, Homosexuality and Nazi Justice', *Journal of Contemporary History*, 27 (41), 1992, p. 47.

30 Ibid., p. 46.

31 For more information, visit the 'Holocaust Encyclopedia' on the

United States Holocaust Memorial Museum website at: http://www.ushmm.org/wlc/en/article.php?ModuleId=10005261.

32 Lautmann, Rüdiger, 'The Pink Triangle: The Persecution of Homosexual Males in Concentration Camps in Nazi Germany', *Journal of Homosexuality*, 1980–1 6, pp. 141–60.

33 Ibid.

34 East Germany decriminalised same-sex activity between men in 1968. West Germany did so the following year. Taffet, David, 'Pink triangle: Even after World War II, gay victims of Nazis continued to be persecuted', *Dallas Voice*, 20 January 2011. Accessed via the *Dallas Voice* website: http://www.dallasvoice.com/pink-triangle-wwii-gay-victims-nazis-continued-persecuted-1061488.html.

35 Nardi, Peter and Bolton, Ralph, 'Gay-Bashing: Violence and aggression against gay men and lesbians' in *Targets of Violence and Aggression*, edited by Ronald Baenninger (New York: Elsevier, 1991), p. 353.

36 Setterington, Ken, *Branded by the Pink Triangle* (Toronto: Second Story Press, 2013), p. 131.

37 Naphy, p. 251.

38 Phillips, Michael, 'The Lobotomy Files: Forgotten Soldiers', *The Wall Street Journal*, 11 December 2013. Accessed via *The Wall Street Journal* website: http://projects.wsj.com/lobotomyfiles/.

39 As quoted in Ordover, Nancy, *American Eugenics: Race, Queer Anatomy, and the Science of Nationalism* (Minneapolis: University of Minnesota Press, 2003), p. 106.

40 American Psychiatric Association, 'Diagnostic and Statistical Manual Mental Disorders' (Washington DC: American Psychiatric Association Mental Hospital Service, 1952).

41 'Employment of Homosexuals and Other Sex Perverts in Government', Subcommittee on Investigations, Committee on Expenditures in the Executive Departments (1950). Accessed via the PBS website: http://www.pbs.org/wgbh/pages/frontline/shows/assault/context/employment.html.

42 Johnson, David K., *The Lavender Scare* (Chicago: University of Chicago Press, 2004), pp. 123–4.

43 SCOCAL, Vallerga v. Dept. Alcoholic Bev. Control, 53 Cal. 2d 313, 347 P.2d 909, 1 Cal. Rptr. 494. Available at: http://scocal.stanford.edu/opinion/vallerga-v-dept-alcoholic-bev-control-29822.

44 *Time*, 'Essay: The Homosexual in America', 21 January 1966. Accessed via the *Time* website: http://content.time.com/time/magazine/article/0,9171,835069,00.html.

45 Hailsham, V., 'Homosexuality and Society', in *They Stand Apart: A critical survey of the problems of homosexuality*, edited by J. T. Rees and H. V. Usill (London: William Heinemann, 1955), pp. 21–35.

46 BBC News, '1957: Homosexuality "should not be a crime"', 4 September 2005. Accessed via the BBC News website: http://news.bbc.co.uk/onthisday/hi/dates/stories/september/4/newsid_3007000/3007686.stm.

47 Lelyveld, Joseph, 'Forster's *Maurice* Becomes a Movie', *New York Times,* 12 November 1986. Accessed via *The New York Times* website: http://www.nytimes.com/1986/11/12/movies/forster-s-maurice-becomes-a-movie.html.

48 Personal communication (12 November 2013).

49 Carter, David, *Stonewall: The Riots that Sparked the Gay Revolution* (New York: St Martin's, 2004), p. 148.

50 Truscott, Lucian, 'Gay Power Comes to Sheridan Square', *The Village Voice*, 3 July 1969, p. 1. Accessed via the website: http://news.google.com/newspapers?id=uuwjAAAAIBAJ&sjid=K4wDAAAAIBAJ&pg=6710,4693&dq=stonewall+inn&hl=en.

51 Di Brienza, Ronnie, 'Stonewall Incident', *East Village Other* 4, No. 32, 9 July 1969, as quoted in Carter, p. 143.

52 Bone, Ruan, 'Julian: A New Series', *Lunch*, September 1972, p. 3.

53 Russell, A. S., 'Spot the Poofter', *Lunch*, September 1972, p. 16.

54 'Profile – David Hockney', *Lunch*, September 1972, p. 5.

55 See Kissack, Terence, 'Freaking Fag Revolutionaries: New York's Gay Liberation Front, 1969–1971', *Radical History Review*, Spring 1995 (62), pp. 105–34. For more information on Britain's early gay liberation movement, see Robinson, Lucy, 'Three Revolutionary Years: The Impact of the Counter Culture on the Development of the Gay Liberation Movement in Britain', *Cultural and Social History*, October 2006, Vol. 3 (4), pp. 445–71 (27).

56 See Fejes, Fred and Petrich, Kevin, 'Invisibility, homophobia and heterosexism: Lesbians, Gays and the Media,' *Review and Criticism*, December 1993, p. 402. The media dealt with homosexuality in a 'less condemnatory way' during the early 1970s. As Fejes et al. point

out, a chronology of *The New York Times* news story abstracts from 1969 to 1975 revealed 'that the majority of entries on homosexuality deal with the issues of expanding rights and gaining greater social acceptance for gays and lesbians'.

57 Rizzo, Domenico, 'Public Spheres and Gay Politics since the Second World War' in *Gay Life and Culture: A World History*, edited by Robert Aldrich (London: Thames & Hudson, 2006), p. 217.

58 Ibid. See also Lewis, Gregory B., 'Lifting the Ban on Gays in the Civil Service: Federal Policy Toward Gay and Lesbian Employees since the Cold War', *Public Administration Review*, September–October 1977, Vol. 57, No. 5, pp. 387–95.

59 Rizzo, p. 220.

60 *EastEnders*, BBC, 1987.

61 Michael Cashman attributes this to *The Star* in Cashman, Michael, 'We had death threats and bricks thrown at us, now it's all so different', *The Mirror*, 25 September 2003. Accessed via: http://www.thefreelibrary. com/We+had+death+threats+and+bricks+thrown+at+us.. now+it's+all+so...-a0108125395.

62 Ibid.

63 Jones, Owen, 'One day "coming out" won't be a thing – and the reaction to Tom Daley's announcement shows we're getting there', *The Independent*, 2 December 2013. Accessed via *The Independent* website: http://www.independent.co.uk/voices/comment/one-day-coming-out-wont-be-a-thing--and-the-reaction-to-tom-daleys-announcement-shows-were-getting-there-8977908.html.

64 Personal communication (10 January 2014).

65 Rose, Lacey, 'The Booming Business of Ellen DeGeneres: From Broke and Banished to Daytime's Top Earner', *The Hollywood Reporter*, 22 August 2012. Accessed via *The Hollywood Reporter* website: http://www.hollywoodreporter.com/news/ellen-degeneres-show-oprah-winfrey-jay-leno-364373?page=2.

66 Handy, Bruce, 'Television: He Called Me Ellen Degenerate?', *Time* magazine, 14 April 1997. Accessed via the *Time* website: http://www.time.com/time/subscriber/article/0,33009,986189-2,00.html.

67 'Now for a queer question about gay culture', *The Economist*, 10 July 1997. Accessed via *The Economist* website: http://www.economist. com/node/370660/print.

68 Prono, Luca, *Encyclopedia of Gay and Lesbian Popular Culture* (Westport: Greenwood Publishing Group, 2008), p. 287.

69 GLAAD, 'Where Are We on TV: 2012–2013 Season', October 2012, p. 3. Available at: http://www.glaad.org/files/whereweareontv12.pdf.

70 Formerly known as the Gay & Lesbian Alliance Against Defamation, the American media monitoring organisation changed its name to GLAAD in 2013 to incorporate bisexual and transgender people into its mission.

71 GLAAD, pp. 3–4.

72 Hewlett, Sylvia Ann; Sears, Todd; Sumberg, Karen; Fargnoli, Christina, 'The Power of Out 2.0: LGBT in the workplace', Center for Talent Innovation, 2013, p. 4, based on 2011 data from the Pew Research Center.

73 Marsh, Stefanie, 'Ian McKellen on Tom Daley, *The Hobbit* and Gandalf's sexuality', *The Times* (of London), 7 December 2013. Accessed via *The Times* website: http://www.thetimes.co.uk/tto/arts/film/article3941753.ece.

74 According to the Human Dignity Trust, seventy-seven countries criminalised homosexuality at the end of 2013. Six other entities also did. These were: the Cook Islands, a self-governing state in free association with New Zealand; the Palestinian Territory; the self-declared state of the Turkish Republic of Northern Cyprus; and the provinces of South Sumatra and Aceh in Indonesia. The status of criminalisation in Iraq and Lesotho is not clear, which means that gay people there face the risk of prosecution. Accounting for these entities, homosexuality is illegal in eighty-six jurisdictions. The death penalty is still in place in Iran, Saudi Arabia, Sudan, Yemen and Mauritania, as well as parts of Nigeria and Somalia.

75 The documentary *Call Me Kuchu* chronicles the final year in the life of Ugandan gay rights activist David Kato, who was bludgeoned to death with a hammer for being gay. See Adams, William Lee, 'Out in Africa', *Attitude*, November 2012, p. 142.

76 Ibid.

77 Verkaiklaw, Robert, 'Iran is safe for "discreet" gays, says Jacqui Smith', *The Independent*, 23 June 2008. Accessed via *The Independent* website: http://www.independent.co.uk/news/uk/politics/iran-is-safe-for-discreet-gays-says-jacqui-smith-852336.html.

78 Personal communication (18 June 2013).

79 'The Global Divide on Homosexuality: Greater Acceptance in More Secular and Affluent Countries', Pew Research Center, Washington DC, 4 June 2013, p. 1.

80 'Putin signs "gay propaganda" ban and law criminalizing insult of religious feelings', *Russia Today*, 30 June 2013. Accessed via the *Russia Today* website: http://on.rt.com/yzvrz4.

81 'Vladimir Putin signs anti-gay propaganda bill', AFP, 30 June 2013. Accessed via *The Telegraph* website: http://www.telegraph.co.uk/news/worldnews/europe/russia/10151790/Vladimir-Putin-signs-anti-gay-propaganda-bill.html.

82 Fierstein, Harvey, 'Russia's Anti-Gay Crackdown', *The New York Times*, 21 July 2013. Accessed via *The New York Times* website: http://www.nytimes.com/2013/07/22/opinion/russias-anti-gay-crackdown.html.

83 'Mr. Putin's War on Gays', editorial, *The New York Times*, 27 July 2013. Accessed via *The New York Times* website: www.nytimes.com/2013/07/28/opinion/sunday/mr-putins-war-on-gays.html?_r=0.

84 Ibid.

85 Fierstein, 2013.

86 Horsey, David, 'Putin's anti-gay laws set the stage for an international battle', *Los Angeles Times*, 15 August 2013. Accessed via the *LA Times* website: http://articles.latimes.com/2013/aug/15/nation/la-na-tt-putins-antigay-laws-20130814.

87 Idov, Michael, 'Putin's "war on gays" is a desperate search for scapegoats', *New Statesman*, 19 August 2013. Accessed via the *New Statesman* website: http://www.newstatesman.com/2013/08/putins-war-gays-desperate-search-scapegoats.

88 Greenhouse, Emily, 'Homophobia in Russia Finds a New Medium', *The New Yorker*, 16 August 2013. Accessed via *The New Yorker* website: http://www.newyorker.com/online/blogs/elements/2013/08/the-rise-of-homophobic-cyberbullying-in-russia.html.

89 Baker, Peter, 'Obama Names Gay Athletes to U.S. Delegation', *The New York Times*, 17 December 2013. Accessed via *The New York Times* website: http://www.nytimes.com/2013/12/18/sports/olympics/obama-names-gay-athletes-to-delegation.html?_r=0.

90 Secretary-General's video message to the Oslo Conference on Human Rights, Sexual Orientation and Gender Identity, 15 April 2013. Accessed via the UN website: http://www.un.org/sg/statements/?nid=6736.

91   Personal communication (2 December 2013).

CHAPTER 3: DEEPLY HIDDEN

1   British Social Attitudes Survey 30. Accessed via the BSA website: http://www.bsa-30.natcen.ac.uk/read-the-report/personal-relationships/homosexuality.aspx.

2   British Social Attitudes Survey, as quoted in Clements, Ben, 'Attitudes Towards Gay Rights', University of Leicester, Institute for Social Change, British Religion in Numbers Website, May 2012. Accessed on 10 December 2013: http://www.brin.ac.uk/figures/attitudes-towards-gay-rights/.

3   The final vote was 390 to 148; see 'Gay Marriage bill: Peers back government plans', BBC News, 5 June 2013. Accessed via the BBC News website: www.bbc.co.uk/news/uk-politics-22764954.

4   'Cameron Warns Europe Rebels: I Won't Budge', Sky News, 22 May 2013. Accessed via the Sky News website: http://news.sky.com/story/1094227/cameron-warns-europe-rebels-i-wont-budge.

5   According to the Pew Research Center, the percentage of people in the United Kingdom who believe that homosexuality should be accepted by society grew from 71 per cent to 76 per cent from 2007 to 2013. Other countries that demonstrated increased acceptance include Italy (65 per cent to 74 per cent), Spain (82 per cent to 88 per cent) and Germany (81 per cent to 87 per cent). See 'The Global Divide on Homosexuality: Greater Acceptance in More Secular and Affluent Countries', Pew Research Center, 4 June 2013, p. 2.

6   The seven polls were conducted by the following polling firms on the following dates: CBS News (8 February 2013), PRRI / Brookings (10 February 2013), Quinnipiac (1 March 2013), ABC News / The Washington Post (9 March 2013), Pew Research (15 March 2013), CNN (16 March 2013) and Fox News (18 March 2013). An eighth poll conducted by Fox News on 26 February 2013 found an equal percentage of people in favour and opposed to same-sex marriage. See Silver, Nate, 'How Opinion on Same-Sex Marriage is Changing, and What It Means', The New York Times, 26 March 2013. Accessed via The New York Times website: http://fivethirtyeight.blogs.nytimes.com/2013/03/26/how-opinion-on-same-sex-marriage-is-changing-and-what-it-means/?_r=0.

7   Belkin, Aaron; Ender, Morten; Frank, Nathaniel; Furia, Stacie; Lucas, George R; Packard, Gary Jr.; Schultz, Tammy S.; Samuels, Steven M.; Segal, David R., 'One Year Out: An Assessment of DADT Repeal's Impact on Military Readiness', 20 September 2012, p. 43.

8   Human Rights Campaign, *Corporate Equality Index 2014*.

9   Hewlett, Sylvia Ann; Sears, Todd; Sumberg, Karen; Fargnoli, Christina. In the US, the authors conducted their study in conjunction with Knowledge Networks, a polling, social science and market research firm that has a large database of potential respondents whom it has recruited online. Knowledge Networks has demographic and other information about each of these respondents. For The Power of Out studies, the firm was able to select people self-identifying as LGBT to participate in the survey. They then applied weights to the data to make it roughly representative of Americans aged twenty-one to sixty-two who are currently employed in white-collar occupations, and have at least a bachelor's degree. The weights used were: age, sex, race/ethnicity, household Internet access, metro status (i.e. whether or not living in an urban area) and region. The weights are essentially derived from the US census, which enables them to provide a reasonable estimate of the population they are trying to capture. Any comparisons repeated here are statistically significant.

10   Noble, Barbara Presley, 'At Work; The Unfolding of Gay Culture', *The New York Times*, 27 June 1993. Accessed via *The New York Times* website: http://www.nytimes.com/1993/06/27/business/at-work-the-unfolding-of-gay-culture.html.

11   Personal communication (21 May 2013).

12   Personal communication (3 October 2013).

13   Personal communication (15 July 2013).

14   Personal communication (19 July 2013).

15   Guasp, April and Dick, Sam, *Living Together: British attitudes to lesbian, gay and bisexual people in 2012* (Stonewall, 2012), p. 3. For this report, YouGov conducted polling among more than 2,000 people. YouGov recruits respondents online using various advertising techniques and does not attempt to construct a sample that is nationally representative. After the survey is conducted, YouGov then applies weights to each respondent in order to make them approximately representative of the general population, but only in terms of their age, gender, social class and the readership of particular newspapers.

16 Hewlett, Sylvia Ann; Sears, Todd; Sumberg, Karen; Fargnoli, Christina, 'The Power of Out 2.0: LGBT in the workplace', Center for Talent Innovation, 2013, p. 25.

17 Personal communication (5 January 2014).

18 Personal communication (25 June 2013).

19 Personal communication (19 June 2013).

20 Personal communication (26 July 2013).

21 Personal communication (13 August 2013).

22 Macalister, Terry and Carvel, John, 'Diversity drive at BP targets gay staff', *The Guardian*, 20 June 2002. Accessed via *The Guardian* website: www.theguardian.com/uk/2002/jun/20/johncarvel.terrymacalister.

23 According to the Employee Benefit Research Institute, domestic partner benefits 'are benefits that an employer chooses to offer an employee's unmarried partner, whether of the same or opposite sex'. Heterosexual couples in the US have traditionally had access to spousal benefits, such as medical coverage for the husbands and wives of employees, whereas gay couples, who could not legally marry, did not. Publicly traded companies in the US started offering such benefits in the early 1990s. Since 2005, gay couples in the UK have been able to enter civil partnerships, which make them eligible for benefits equivalent to spousal benefits under the law. For more information, see Solomon, Todd A., *Domestic Partner Benefits: An Employer's Guide* (Washington: Thompson, 2006).

24 Dougary, Ginny, 'Lord Browne: I'm much happier now than I've ever been', *The Times* (of London), 6 February 2010. Accessed via *The Times* website: www.thetimes.co.uk/tto/business/moversshakers/article1891575.ece. This *Times* article refers to a quote from an interview with the *Financial Times*, the transcript for which is no longer available online.

25 Pierce, Andrew, 'Lord Browne made atypical misjudgment', *The Telegraph*, 2 May 2007. Accessed via *The Telegraph* website: http://www.telegraph.co.uk/news/uknews/1550281/Lord-Browne-made-atypical-misjudgment.html.

26 Roberts, Laura, '*Desert Island Discs*' most controversial castaways', *The Telegraph*, 2 March 2011. Accessed via *The Telegraph* website: http://www.telegraph.co.uk/culture/tvandradio/8355867/Desert-Island-Discs-most-controversial-castaways.html.

CHAPTER 4: PHANTOMS AND FEARS

1   Personal communication (30 December 2013).

2   By the end of 2013, the House of Representatives had not brought the bill up for a vote.

3   These data are based on the US General Social Survey, which is nationally representative. See Pizer, Jennifer C.; Sears, Brad; Mallory, Christy; and Hunter, Nan D., 'Evidence of Persistent and Pervasive Workplace Discrimination Against LGBT People: The Need for Federal Legislation Prohibiting Discrimination and Providing for Equal Employment Benefits', 2012, 45 Loy. L.A. L. Rev. 715. Available at: http://digitalcommons.lmu.edu/llr/vol45/iss3/3.

4   Hewlett, Sylvia Ann; Sears, Todd; Sumberg, Karen; Fargnoli, Christina, 'The Power of Out 2.0: LGBT in the workplace', Center for Talent Innovation, 2013, p. 4, based on 2011 data from the Pew Research Center.

5   According to the 2012 Alliance for Board Diversity Census, Caucasian men held 73.3 per cent of the more than 5,300 board seats in Fortune 500 companies. Overall, men held 83.4 per cent of board seats and women just 16.6 per cent. Only 13.3 per cent of seats were not held by white men and women. These figures reflect self-reported gender and ethnicity of board members. Data on sexual orientation were not collected. For more information, see 'Missing Pieces: Women and Minorities on *Fortune* 500 Boards', Alliance for Board Diversity, 15 August 2013. Accessed via the Alliance for Board Diversity website: http://theabd.org/2012_ABD%20Missing_Pieces_Final_8_15_13.pdf.

6   The 2013 Spencer Stuart Board Index for the US looked at 493 of the 500 S&P 500 boards. It found that the average age of independent directors increased from 60.3 years in 2003 to 62.9 years in 2013, and that 44 per cent of boards in 2013 had an average age of 64 or older, compared with 14 per cent a decade ago. Accessed via: https://www.spencerstuart.com/~/media/PDF%20Files/Research%20and%20Insight%20PDFs/SSBI-2013_01Nov2013.pdf.

7   Personal communication (19 November 2013).

8   Personal communication (19 November 2013).

9   Personal communication (19 November 2013).

10 Christopher Bailey was appointed chief executive of Burberry in October 2013. When he takes up the role in 2014, he will not become

the first openly gay chief executive to lead a FTSE 100 company. Charles Allen served as chief executive of Granada Group from 1996 to 2000, and as chief executive of ITV from 2004 to 2007. Both companies were constituents of the FTSE 100 during Allen's tenure.

11 Banaji, Mahzarin R. and Greenwald, Anthony G., *Blindspot: Hidden Biases of Good People* (Delacorte Press: New York, 2013), p. xii.

12 Tests can be taken by visiting http://implicit.harvard.edu.

13 Nosek, Brian A. and Riskind, Rachel G., 'Policy implications of implicit social cognition', *Social Issues and Policy Review*, 2012, 6, pp. 112–45.

14 Personal communication (27 September 2013).

15 Tilcsik, A., 'Pride and prejudice: Employment discrimination against openly gay men in the US', *American Journal of Sociology*, 2011, 117 (2), 2011: 586–626.

16 Because both of the résumés were sent to each employer, it was necessary to make them slightly different in order to avoid arousing the suspicions of the employer. However, these differences between résumés should not have affected the results of the study, since references to the 'gay' and 'straight' organisations were randomly assigned to a particular résumé in each case. In addition, the author used regression modelling to check the results for systematic bias between the two résumés, and found that there was no bias.

17 This gap is statistically significant ($p < .001$) and implies that a heterosexual job seeker had to apply to fewer than nine different jobs to receive a positive response, while a gay applicant needed to reply to almost fourteen advertisements to achieve the same result. See Tilcsik, pp. 605–6.

18 See Tilcsik, p. 596. Researchers in other countries have uncovered similar results. In a 2009 study in Greece, researchers sent pairs of résumés to 1,714 private-sector job postings in Athens. They did not explicitly state that one of the candidates was gay, but listed that he had once volunteered for a gay organisation in the personal information section of the résumé. The straight candidate volunteered for an environmental organisation instead. Both applicants were said to be twenty-nine years old and had served in the Greek military. Even so, applicants with gay volunteer experience were 26.2 per cent less likely to receive an interview than their heterosexual counterparts. They were nearly 35 per cent less likely to be invited for an interview

when the manager reviewing applications was male. (Drydakis, Nick, 'Sexual Orientation Discrimination in the Labour Market', *Labour Economics*, 2009, 16: 364–72. Other studies show that this bias applies also to lesbian applicants (Weichselbaumer, Doris, 'Sexual Orientation Discrimination in Hiring', *Labour Economics*, 2003, 10: 629–42).

19 Sears, Brad and Mallory, Christy. 'Documented Evidence of Employment Discrimination and its Effects on LGBT People', The Williams Institute, July 2011. Accessed via: http://williamsinstitute. law.ucla.edu/wp-content/uploads/Sears-Mallory-Discrimination-July-20111.pdf.

20 Laurent, Thierry and Mihoubi, Ferhat, 'Sexual Orientation and Wage Discrimination in France: The Hidden Side of the Rainbow', *Journal of Labor Research*, 2012, 33: 487–527, p. 488.

21 For instance, Jefferson Frank, an economist in London, has found that married heterosexual men in their forties and fifties who worked at British universities earned salaries that were 17 per cent higher than single heterosexual men of the same age, even after controlling for variables such as experience and education. See, Frank, J. (2006), 'Is the male marriage premium evidence of discrimination against gay men?' in *Sexual Orientation Discrimination: An International Perspective* (Routledge: New York, 2007), pp. 93–104.

22 See, for instance, Ginther, Donna K. and Zavodny, Madeline, 'Is the male marriage premium due to selection? The effect of shotgun weddings on the return to marriage', *Journal of Population Economics*, Springer-Verlag, 2001, Vol. 14(2), pp. 313–28.

23 See, for instance, Korenman, S. and Neumark, D., 'Does marriage really make men more productive?', *The Journal of Human Resources*, 1991, 26 (2): 282–307; 'Lundberg, S. and Rose, E., 'The effects of sons and daughters on men's labor supply and wages', *The Review of Economics and Statistics*, 2002, 84 (2): 251–68; Akerlof, George A., 'Men without children', *The Economic Journal*, 1998, 108 (447): 287–309; Becker, Gary S., 'A theory of the allocation of time', *The Economic Journal*, 1965, 75 (299): 493–517.

24 See, for instance, Carpenter, Christopher (2006), 'Do straight men "come out" at work too? The heterosexual male marriage premium and discrimination against gay men' in *Sexual Orientation Discrimination: An International Perspective* (Routledge: New York, 2007), pp. 76–92.

25 Carpenter, a professor at the University of California at Irvine, writes that 'the traditionally conceived marriage premium partly

reflects a reward for sending a heterosexual signal'. See Carpenter (2006), p. 88.

26 Personal communication (11 June 2013).

27 Movement Advancement Project, Human Rights Campaign and Center for American Progress, 'A Broken Bargain: Discrimination, Fewer Benefits and More Taxes for LGBT Workers' (Full Report), June 2013, p. 35.

28 Ibid.

29 Blandford, John, 'The Nexus of Sexual Orientation and Gender in the Determination of Earnings', *Industrial and Labor Relations Review*, 1 July 2003, Vol. 56 (4), p. 640.

30 Movement Advancement Project, p. 35.

31 Personal communication (13 October 2013).

32 Personal communication (26 September 2013).

33 Personal communication (10 October 2013).

34 Personal communication (17 December 2013).

35 Personal communication (26 June 2013).

36 Personal communication (4 July 2013).

37 Grant, Jaime M.; Mottet, Lisa A.; Tanis, Justin; Harrison, Jack; Herman, Jody L.; Keisling, M., *Injustice at Every Turn* (Washington: National Center for Transgender Equality and National Gay and Lesbian Task Force, 2011), p. 3.

38 Personal communication (18 July 2013).

39 Appeals from the US District Court for the Northern District of Georgia, 6 December 2011. Accessed via the US Court of Appeals 11th Circuit website: http://www.ca11.uscourts.gov/opinions/ops/201014833.pdf.

40 Personal communication (7 May 2013).

41 Emails to Replacements Ltd. shared by Bob Page.

42 See the FBI's Hate Crime Statistics web page, available at: http://www.fbi.gov/about-us/cjis/ucr/hate-crime/2011/hate-crime. See also Tzatzev, Aleksi, 'There's a Disturbing Trend Involving Anti-Gay Hate Crime in the US', *Business Insider*, 12 December 2012. Accessed via the Business Insider website: www.businessinsider.com/anti-gay-hate-crime-stats-dont-budge-2012-12.

43 The percentage of people in France who said that homosexuality should be accepted decreased from 83 per cent in 2007 to 77 per cent in 2013. This was the largest absolute decrease of any region polled, including Ghana, the Czech Republic, Poland, Jordan, Russia, Turkey and the Palestinian territories. All of these regions showed a lower percentage accepting homosexuality in 2013 than in 2007. See 'The Global Divide on Homosexuality: Greater Acceptance in More Secular and Affluent Countries,' Pew Research Center, 4 June 2013, p. 2.

44 Sethi, Neeruj, 'France Gay Marriage: Hate Crimes Spike After Bill Passes', PolicyMic, 9 May 2013. Accessed via the PolicyMic website: www.policymic.com/articles/40695/france-gay-marriage-hate-crimes-spike-after-bill-passes.

45 Sacks, Jonathan, *The Dignity of Difference: How to Avoid the Clash of Civilizations* (New York: Continuum, 2002), p. 46.

46 '30% increase in anti-Semitic incidents worldwide in 2012', *The Times of Israel*, 7 April 2013. Accessed via *The Times of Israel* website: http://www.timesofisrael.com/report-finds-30-increase-in-anti-semitic-incidents-worldwide/.

CHAPTER 5: COMING OUT IS GOOD BUSINESS

1 Browne, John, 'Three reasons why I'm voting for gay marriage', *Financial Times*, 2 June 2013.

2 Personal communication (12 July 2013).

3 The San Francisco Chamber of Commerce, Google, H5 and Levi Strauss & Co. filed a join amicus brief on 15 January 2009. Available at: http://www.courts.ca.gov/documents/s1680xx-amcur-sfchamber-commerce.pdf.

4 Eckholm, Erik, 'Corporate Call for Change in Gay Marriage Case', *The New York Times*, 27 February 2013. Accessed via *The New York Times* website: http://www.nytimes.com/2013/02/28/business/companies-ask-justices-to-overturn-gay-marriage-ban.html?_r=0.

5 Amicus Briefs, 278 Employers and Organizations Representing Employers. Accessed at the website: http://www.glad.org/doma/documents/.

6 Garber, Andrew, 'Starbucks supports gay marriage legislation', *The Seattle Times*, 24 January 2012. Accessed via *The Seattle Times* website:

http://seattletimes.com/html/politicsnorthwest/2017323520_starbucks_supports_gay_marriag.html.

7   See the National Organization for Marriage (21 March 2012), 'The National Organization for Marriage Announces International "Dump Starbucks" Protest Campaign' (Press Release). Accessed via the NOM blog: http://www.nomblog.com/20812/#sthash.10x1eaTr.dpbs; and the Dump Starbucks campaign website: http://www.dumpstarbucks.com/.

8   Gilbert, Kathleen, 'Like traditional marriage? Then dump Starbucks, says National Organization for Marriage', LifeSiteNews.com, 29 March 2012. Accessed via the LifeSiteNews.com website: http://www.lifesitenews.com/news/like-traditional-marriage-then-dump-starbucks-says-national-organization-fo/. Facebook likes were accessed via the Dump Starbucks Facebook page: https://www.facebook.com/dumpstarbucks/posts/636562603037541.

9   Allen, Frederick, 'Howard Schultz to Anti-Gay-Marriage Starbucks Shareholder: "You Can Sell Your Shares"', *Forbes* magazine, 22 March 2013. Accessed via the *Forbes* website: http://www.forbes.com/sites/frederickallen/2013/03/22/howard-schultz-to-anti-gay-marriage-starbucks-shareholder-you-can-sell-your-shares/.

10 'Goldman Sachs CEO Lloyd Blankfein: Same-sex marriage support "a business issue"', CBS News, 10 March 2013. Accessed via the CBS News website: http://www.cbsnews.com/news/goldman-sachs-ceo-lloyd-blankfein-same-sex-marriage-support-a-business-issue/.

11 Ibid.

12 Out Now Global LGBT2020 Study (2011), p. 18. Received by personal communication (5 June 2013).

13 Personal communication (13 June 2013).

14 Human Rights Campaign, *Corporate Equality Index 2014*, p. 6.

15 Ibid.

16 For the 2014 figure, see Human Rights Campaign, *Corporate Equality Index 2014*, p. 8. The 2002 figure was confirmed via personal communication with the HRC on 6 January 2014.

17 The first Corporate Equality Index (CEI) survey began by evaluating companies against seven criteria, which still form the basis of the scoring system. It awards them points based on whether they have a written non-discrimination policy covering sexual orientation in the

employee handbook or manual; offer health insurance coverage to same-sex domestic partners; recognise and support an LGBT employee resource group; offer diversity training that includes sexual orientation and gender expression in the workplace; engage in respectful and appropriate marketing to the LGBT community; and provide support to LGBT or AIDS-related organisations. Points are subtracted from a company's score if it acts to undermine equality for LGBT people. To learn more about the evolution of the CEI scoring system, consult the Human Rights Campaign's *Corporate Equality Index 2013*, p. 12.

18   For the 2002 Corporate Equality Index, HRC rated 319 companies. Thirteen of them received perfect scores. See Human Rights Campaign, *Corporate Equality Index 2002*. Accessed via the HRC website: http://www.hrc.org/files/assets/resources/CorporateEqualityIndex_2002.pdf.

19   For the 2011 Corporate Equality Index, HRC rated 615 companies. See Human Rights Campaign, *Corporate Equality Index 2011*. Accessed via the HRC website: http://www.hrc.org/files/assets/resources/CorporateEqualityIndex_2011.pdf.

20   In 2012, Exxon did not meet any of the HRC criteria, and it was docked 25 points for working against shareholder resolutions calling for greater LGBT inclusion. It received a negative score again in 2013 and 2014. See Taffet, David, 'Exxon maintains negative score on annual equality report', *Dallas Voice*, 13 December 2013. Accessed via the *Dallas Voice* website: http://www.dallasvoice.com/exxon-maintains-negative-score-annual-equality-report-10163316.html. See also Juhasz, Antonia, 'What's Wrong with Exxon?', *Advocate*, 3 September 2013. Accessed via the *Advocate* website: http://www.advocate.com/print-issue/current-issue/2013/09/03/whats-wrong-exxon.

21   Human Rights Campaign, *Corporate Equality Index 2005*. Accessed via the HRC website: http://www.hrc.org/files/assets/resources/CorporateEqualityIndex_2005.pdf.

22   Human Rights Campaign. *Corporate Equality Index 2006*. Accessed via the HRC website: http://www.hrc.org/files/assets/resources/CorporateEqualityIndex_2006.pdf.

23   Personal communication (21 June 2013).

24   See, for example, this exhaustive review of thirty-six research studies on the impact of LGBT-supportive policies and working environments on business outcomes: Badgett, M. V. Lee; Durso, Laura E.; Mallory,

Christy; Kastanis, Angeliki, 'The Business Impact of LGBT-Supportive Workplace Policies', The Williams Institute, May 2013.

25 Personal communication (18 June 2013).

26 Personal communication (10 July 2013).

27 Sears, B. and Mallory, C. 'Economic motives for adopting LGBT-related workplace policies', 2011. Accessed via The Williams Institute website: http://williamsinstitute.law.ucla.edu/wp-content/uploads/Mallory-Sears-Corp-Statements-Oct2011.pdf.

28 Hewlett, Sylvia Ann; Sears, Todd; Sumberg, Karen; Fargnoli, Christina, 'The Power of Out 2.0: LGBT in the workplace', Center for Talent Innovation, 2013, p. 30.

29 A lack of policies to protect them was cited by 18 per cent of respondents, while 17 per cent reported a fear of getting fired. Human Rights Campaign, *Degrees of equality: A national study examining workplace climate for LGBT employees*, 2009, p. 15. Accessed via the Human Rights Campaign website: https://www.hrc.org/files/assets/resources/DegreesOfEquality_2009.pdf.

30 Ibid., p. 13.

31 Hewlett, Sylvia Ann and Sumberg, Karen, 'The Power of Out', Center for Work-Life Policy, 2011, p. 7. The Center for Work-Life Policy is now the Center for Talent Innovation.

32 Personal communication (3 December 2013).

33 Everly, B. A.; Shih, M. J.; and Ho, G. C., 'Don't ask, don't tell? Does disclosure of gay identity affect partner performance?', *Journal of Experimental Social Psychology*, January 2012, Vol. 48, Issue 1, pp. 407–10. Two separate experiments were conducted. In the first, study participants sat in a room where another participant was already waiting for the study to begin. Participants were given a sheet describing their partner in the task. In the 'ambiguous' condition, they were told that their partner came from San Francisco, studied interior design and enjoyed cooking and dancing. They were told that he was in a relationship, but the gender of his partner was not revealed. In the 'disclosed' condition, participants received identical information about their study partner, but were told that he was in a relationship with a man named Josh. Participants and their study partner, a student portrayed by a gay man, then completed a mathematics test. As predicted, participants paired with the openly gay partner outperformed their counterparts. In the second

experiment, the authors tested performance in a video game task that required sustained interaction between participants as they attempted to shoot targets on a screen. Once again, participants paired with openly gay partners scored significantly higher.

34 Ibid., p. 409.

35 Personal communication (10 June 2013).

36 Out & Equal Workplace Advocates, Harris Interactive and Witeck Combs Communications (2006), 'Majority of Americans: Companies not government should decide benefits offered to same-sex employees' (press release), 22 May 2006. Accessed via the Out & Equal website: http://outandequal.org/documents/2006_Workplace_Survey052306.pdf.

37 Ibid.

38 See Florida, Richard, *The Rise of the Creative Class* (New York: Basic Books, 2002) and Florida, Richard, *The Flight of the Creative Class* (New York: Harper Business, 2005).

39 Gates, Gary and Florida, Richard, 'Technology and Tolerance: The Importance of Diversity to High-Technology Growth', the Brookings Institution, June 2001. Accessed via the Brookings Institution website: http://www.brookings.edu/research/reports/2001/6/technology-florida.

40 These cities are San Francisco, Washington DC, Austin, Atlanta and San Diego.

41 Florida, Richard, 'Gay-tolerant societies prosper economically', *USA Today*, 30 April 2003. Accessed via the *USA Today* website: http://usatoday30.usatoday.com/news/opinion/editorials/2003-04-30-florida_x.htm.

42 Noland, Marcus, 'Popular Attitudes, Globalization, and Risk', July 2004. Accessed via the website: http://www.iie.com/publications/wp/wp04-2.pdf.

43 Noland, M., 'Tolerance Can Lead to Prosperity', *Financial Times*, 18 August 2004. Accessed via the Peterson Institute for International Economics website: http://www.iie.com/publications/opeds/oped.cfm?ResearchID=216.

44 Inglehart, R.; Foa, R.; Peterson, C.; Welzel, C., 'Development, Freedom, and Rising Happiness: A Global Perspective (1981–2007)', *Perspectives on Psychological Science*, 2008, Vol. 3 (4), p. 269.

45 See, for instance, Bosson, J. K.; Weaver, J. R.; Prewitt-Freilino, J. L., 'Concealing to Belong, Revealing to be Known: Classification Expectations and Self-threats Among Persons with Concealable Stigmas', *Self and Identity*, 2012, Vol. 11 (1), pp. 114–35 ; Smart, Laura and Wegner, Daniel M., 'Covering up what can't be seen: Concealable stigma and mental control', *Journal of Personality and Social Psychology*, September 1999, Vol. 77(3), pp. 474–86.

46 Snyder, Kirk, *The G Quotient* (San Francisco: Jossey-Bass, 2006).

47 Ibid, p. xx. See also Odets, Walt, 'Some Thoughts on Gay Male Relationships and American Society', *Journal of the Gay and Lesbian Medical Association,* Fall 1998, Vol. 2 (1).

48 See Nicholas, Cheryl L., 'Gaydar: Eye-gaze as identity recognition among gay men and lesbians', *Sexuality and Culture*, Winter 2004, Vol. 8 (1), pp. 60–86; and Adams, William Lee, 'Finely Tuned Gaydar' (letter to the editor), *The New York Times*, 26 June 2005. Accessed via the *The New York Times* website: http://www.nytimes.com/2005/06/26/fashion/sundaystyles/26LETTERS.html?_r=0.

49 This style includes seven principles of leadership: inclusion, creativity, adaptability, connectivity, communication, intuition and collaboration. Snyder describes them collectively as the 'G Quotient'.

50 Personal communication (18 June 2013).

51 'Send an email to Campbell Soup Company President Douglas Conant. Tell him you want his company to stop supporting the gay agenda', 19 December 2009. Accessed via the American Family Association website: http://www.afa.net/Detail.aspx?id=2147483667.

52 Personal communication (27 June 2013).

53 Harris Interactive (18 November 2013). 'America's LGBT 2013 Buying Power Estimated at $830 Billion' (press release).

54 Personal communication with Witeck Communications (20 June 2013), who works in partnership with Harris Interactive.

55 Wheeler-Quinnell, Charlotte, *Marketing: How to Market to Gay Consumers* (Stonewall Workplace Guides, 2010).

56 Personal communication (30 December 2013).

57 Harris Interactive, 'Large Majorities of Heterosexuals and Gays Likely to Consider a Corporate Brand that Provides Equal Workplace Benefits to All Employees, Including Gay and Lesbian Employees' (press release), 6 February 2007. Accessed via the

Harris Interactive website: http://www.harrisinteractive.com/NEWS/allnewsbydate.asp?NewsID=1171.

58   Personal communication (20 June 2013).

59   Personal communication (13 June 2013).

60   Personal communication (3 June 2013).

61   Personal communication (2 October 2013).

CHAPTER 6: THE BENEFITS OF COMING OUT

1   Personal communication (19 August 2013).

2   Personal communication (2 July 2013).

3   Reid-Smith, Tris, 'Global business leader Beth Brooke on coming out gay', *Gay Star News*, 20 April 2012. Accessed via the *Gay Star News* website: http://www.gaystarnews.com/article/global-business-leader-beth-brooke-coming-out-gay200412#sthash.B5Z5K32L.dpuf.

4   Personal communication (20 June 2013).

5   Antonio Simoes is CEO UK and European head of retail banking and wealth management at HSBC.

6   Personal communication (14 August 2013).

7   Personal communication (15 August 2013).

8   Black, Kathryn N. and Stevenson, Michael R., 'The relationship of self-reported sex-role characteristics and attitudes toward homosexuality', *Journal of Homosexuality,* 1984, Vol. 10 (1–2), pp. 83–93.

9   Research consistently indicates that heterosexual men view gay men more negatively than they view lesbians. See Kite, Mary. E. and Whitely, Bernard E., Jr., 'Sex difference in attitudes toward homosexual persons, behaviors, and civil rights: A meta-analysis', *Personality and Social Psychology Bulletin*, 1996, 22 (4), pp. 336–53, and Herek, Gregory M., 'Sexual prejudice and gender: Do heterosexuals' attitudes toward lesbians and gay men differ?', *Journal of Social Issues*, 2000, 56 (2), pp. 251–66. As Herek writes in the latter article, '… heterosexual men's attitudes toward gay men are consistently more hostile than their attitudes toward lesbians or heterosexual women's attitudes toward homosexuals of either gender'. Herek has also written that for heterosexual men 'the topic of homosexuality often activates considerations of sexuality, gender identity and personal threat, which are likely to

evoke a defensive function'. See Herek, Gregory M. and Capitanio, J. P., 'Sex differences in how heterosexuals think about lesbians and gay men: Evidence from survey context effects', *The Journal of Sex Research*, 1999, 36, pp. 348–60.

10   Personal communication (13 June 2013).

11   Personal communication (11 July 2013).

12   Personal communication (21 June 2013).

13   Human Rights Campaign, *Degrees of equality: A national study examining workplace climate for LGBT employees*, 2009, p. 15.

14   Ibid.

15   Personal communication (13 June 2013).

16   Personal communication (27 June 2013).

17   Personal communication (10 June 2013).

18   Personal communication (7 August 2013).

19   Personal communication (30 October 2013).

CHAPTER 7: OPINION FORMERS AND ICONS

1   Personal communication (2 September 2013).

2   Miranda Curtis was appointed chairman of Waterstones in October 2011. Stephen Clarke became chief executive of WHSmith in July 2013.

3   Personal communication (6 June 2013).

4   Personal communication (19 November 2013).

5   Personal communication (1 October 2013).

6   For more information on openly gay elected officials, visit the Victory Fund website at http://victoryfund.org.

7   It is well established that incumbency is a major hurdle for new politicians in the US. This might explain the relatively slower pace of change in the US compared to the UK. See, for instance, Cox, Gary W. and Katz, Jonathan N., 'Why Did the Incumbency Advantage in the U.S. House Elections Grow?', *American Journal of Political Science*, May 1996, Vol. 40 (2), pp. 478–97; and Uppal, Yogesh, 'Estimating Incumbency Effects in U.S. State *Legislatures*: A Quasi-Experimental Study', *Economics & Politics*, 2010, 22, pp. 180–99.

8   Faiola, Anthony, 'Sicily's first openly gay governor wins support with anti-mafia crusade', *The Washington Post*, 2 August 2013. Accessed via *The Washington Post* website: http://articles.washingtonpost.com/2013-08-02/world/40999023_1_cosa-nostra-mafia-nichi-vendola.

9   Reynolds, Andrew, *Out in Office: LGBT Legislators and LGBT Rights Around the World* (Chapel Hill: LGBT Representation and Rights Initiative, 2013), pp. 29–33.

10   Ibid.

11   This is in contrast to 1.5 per cent of surveyed adults who identified themselves as gay, lesbian or bisexual in 2012. See Office for National Statistics, 'Key Findings from the Integrated Household Survey, January to December 2012'. Available at: http://www.ons.gov.uk/ons/dcp171778_329407.pdf. The survey gathered data from approximately 340,000 individuals, making it the largest pool of UK social data after the census. Citizens of the UK elect 650 Members of Parliament to represent their interests in the House of Commons. At the end of 2013, twenty-four were gay, representing 3.5 per cent of the body.

12   Members of Parliament split their time between their home constituencies and the Houses of Parliament in London. Parliamentary rules allow them to claim expenses for maintaining second homes. Since 2006, the rules have prohibited MPs from paying rent to their partners. In May 2010, Laws resigned from his position as Chief Secretary to the Treasury after a newspaper published a report that he had claimed more than £40,000 in expenses for rent paid to his partner. Laws said that he had hoped claiming expenses would help keep his sexual orientation private and that he did not seek to maximise personal profit.

13   On 15 July 2010, *The Guardian* published an editorial that I wrote expressing my sadness that a public figure like David Laws felt the need to hide his sexuality. See 'Being outed is a blessing', *The Guardian*, 15 July 2010.

14   Personal communication (8 July 2013).

15   'Profile: Berlin's cult-status mayor', BBC News, 22 October 2001. Accessed via the BBC website: http://news.bbc.co.uk/1/hi/world/europe/1613270.stm.

16   *Hansard*, Vol. 124, cc. 987–1038, House of Commons debate, 15 December 1987. Accessed via the *Hansard* website: http://hansard.millbanksystems.com/sittings/1987/dec/15/prohibition-on-promoting-homosexuality.

17   Personal communication (25 September 2013).

18   Savage, Michael, 'Gay Tory MP Crispin Blunt fights off local "dinosaurs" who tried to oust him', *The Times*, 19 November 2013. Accessed via *The Times* website: http://www.thetimes.co.uk/tto/news/politics/article3925282.ece.

19   'The Global Divide on Homosexuality: Creates Acceptance in More Secular and Affluent Countries,' Pew Research Center, Washington DC, 4 June 2013.

20   CBOS Public Opinion Research Center, 'Polish Public Opinion', February 2013. Accessed via the CBOS website: http://www.cbos.pl/PL/publikacje/public_opinion/2013/02_2013.pdf.

21   Gera, Vanessa, 'Lech Walesa Shocks Poland with Anti-Gay Words', *Huffington Post*, 3 March 2013. Accessed via *The Huffington Post* website: http://www.huffingtonpost.com/2013/03/03/lech-walesa-shocks-poland_n_2802860.html.

22   Personal communication (25 September 2013).

23   'Krystyna Pawlowicz mocks Anna Grodzka', *Super Express*, 29 January 2013. Accessed via the *Super Express* website: http://www.se.pl/wydarzenia/kraj/krystyna-pawlowicz-kpi-z-anny-grodzkiej-blaszczak-brakujej-jej-doswiadczenia_303820.html.

24   Personal communication (1 October 2013).

25   'Soccer chief calls for gays to come out', Associated Press, 17 January 2012. Accessed via the ESPN website: http://espn.go.com/sports/soccer/news/_/id/7471041/german-soccer-chief-theo-zwanziger-calls-gays-come-out.

26   These are Major League Baseball, the National Basketball Association, the National Football League and the National Hockey League.

27   According to the UEFA rankings, the top six soccer leagues in Europe are Spain's La Liga, the English Premier League, Germany's Bundesliga, Italy's Serie A, Portugal's Primeira Liga and France's Ligue 1. Accessed via the UEFA website: http://www.uefa.com/memberassociations/uefarankings/country/.

28   'Inner strength, inner peace', Associated Press, 2 November 1994. Accessed via the website: http://news.google.com/newspapers?id=tplQAAAAIBAJ&sjid=FRMEAAAAIBAJ&pg=2309%2C370004.

29   Personal communication (13 December 2013).

30 'Homosexualität wird im Fußball ignoriert', *Die Zeit*, 13 January 2014. Accessed via the *Die Zeit* website: http://www.zeit.de/2014/03/homosexualitaet-profifussball-thomas-hitzlsperger.

31 'Thomas Hitzlsperger: Former Aston Villa player reveals he is gay', BBC News, 8 January 2014. Accessed via the BBC News website: http://www.bbc.co.uk/sport/0/football/25628806.

32 Starr Seibel, Deborah, 'Billie Jean King recalls women's rights struggle of her time', *New York Post*, 31 August 2013. Accessed via the *New York Post* website: nypost.com/2013/08/31/sports-legend-billie-jean-king-recalls-womens-rights-struggle-of-her-time/.

33 Personal communication (1 October 2013).

34 Wertheim, Jon, 'A reluctant trailblazer, Navratilova laid groundwork for Collins', *Sports Illustrated*, 30 April 2013. Accessed via the *Sports Illustrated* website: http://sportsillustrated.cnn.com/magazine/news/20130430/jason-collins-martina-navratilova/.

35 Personal communication (1 October 2013).

36 Adams, William Lee, 'Olympic Homophobia: Why Are There So Few Openly Gay Athletes?', *Time* magazine, 9 August 2012. Accessed via the *Time* website: olympics.time.com/2012/08/09/olympic-homophobia-why-are-there-so-few-openly-gay-athletes/.

37 'Jason Collins says he's gay', ESPN.com, 30 April 2013. Accessed via the ESPN website: http://espn.go.com/nba/story/_/id/9223657/.

38 Brinson, Will, 'Brendon Ayanbadejo, Chris Kluwe file brief supporting gay marriage', CBS.com, 28 February 2013. Accessed via the CBS Sports website: http://www.cbssports.com/nfl/eye-on-football/21787786/brendon-ayanbadejo-chris-kluwe-file-amicus-brief-supporting-gay-marriage.

39 Personal communication (9 October 2013).

40 Personal communication (13 December 2013).

41 BBC News, 'Olympic diving star Tom Daley in relationship with man', 2 December 2013. Accessed via the BBC News website: www.bbc.co.uk/news/uk-england-devon-25183041.

42 *The World at One*, BBC Radio 4, 2 December 2013.

43 Personal communication (11 July 2013).

44 Barry, Dan, 'A Sports Executive Leaves the Safety of His Shadow Life', *The New York Times*, 15 May 2011. Accessed via *The New York*

Times website: www.nytimes.com/2011/05/16/sports/basketball/
nba-executive-says-he-is-gay.html?pagewanted=all&_r=0.

45 Fulford, Adrian, Diversity Speech, South East Circuit, Middle
Temple Hall, 20 January 2009. Accessed via the website: www.
judiciary.gov.uk/Resources/JCO/Documents/Speeches/justice-
fulford-diversity-middle-temple-hall-200109.pdf.

46 Personal communication (9 October 2013).

47 Ibid.

48 Personal communication (9 October 2013).

49 LGB Solicitor Career Survey 2009/2010, InterLaw Diversity Forum
for LGBT Networks. Accessed via the website: http://outandequal.
org/documents/London%20Calling.pdf.

50 Personal communication (24 September 2013).

51 Burton, Lucy, 'Revealed: females make up less than 10 per cent of
top 100's equity partner ranks', *The Lawyer*, 24 October 2012.
Accessed via *The Lawyer* website: http://www.thelawyer.com/
revealed-females-make-up-less-than-10-per-cent-of-top-100s-
equity-partner-ranks/1015190.article.

52 Hall, Kathleen, 'Diversity League Table shows promotion gap', *The
Law Society Gazette*, 11 November 2013. Accessed via the *Law Gazette*
website: http://www.lawgazette.co.uk/law/diversity-league-table-
shows-promotion-gap/5038711.article.

53 LGB Solicitor Career Survey 2009/2010.

54 Personal communication (27 September 2013).

CHAPTER 8: SHATTERING THE GLASS

1 Personal communication (6 September 2013).

2 On 10 December 2013, Auburn University's College of Human
Sciences awarded Tim Cooke, a 1982 graduate of the college, a
lifetime achievement award. Cook's remarks came during his
acceptance speech, which Auburn uploaded to its official YouTube
channel on 14 December 2013. The video is available at: http://
youtu.be/dNEafGCf-kw.

3 Personal communication (14 August 2013).

4 'Out on the Street 2013: A Message from the Founder'. Accessed

via the website: http://outonthestreet.org/wp-content/uploads/2012/11/membership-overview.pdf.

5   Personal communication (12 July 2013).

6   Kwoh, Leslie, 'Firms Hail New Chiefs (of Diversity)', *The Wall Street Journal*, 5 January 2012. Accessed via *The Wall Street Journal* website: http://online.wsj.com/article/SB10001424052970203899504577129261732884578.html.

7   Dexter, Billy, 'The Chief Diversity Officer Today: Inclusion Gets Down to Business', Heidrick and Struggles, 2010. Accessed via the Toronto Region immigrant Employment Council website: http://triec.ca/uploads/344/inclusion_gets_down_to_business_cdo_summ.pdf.

8   Kwoh, 2012.

9   Personal communication (11 September 2013).

10   Personal communication (17 September 2013).

11   'IBM Supplier Conduct Principles: Guidelines'. Accessed via the Human Rights Campaign website: http://www.hrc.org/files/assets/resources/scpg-v2.0.pdf. In 2004, the National Gay and Lesbian Chamber of Commerce (NGLCC) joined forces with eleven corporations, including American Airlines, IBM, Intel and JPMorgan Chase, to found the Supplier Diversity Initiative. The programme certifies small businesses as LGBTBEs (lesbian, gay, bisexual and transgender business enterprises), businesses that are majority owned, operated and managed by LGBT people. Certification helps businesses stand out in procurement processes and allows corporations to identify legitimate LGBT businesses with which to work.

12   Personal communication (10 June 2013).

13   Personal communication (16 January 2014).

14   'Gayglers: Google's LGBT Employee Resource Group'. Accessed via the Google blog: http://googleblog.blogspot.co.uk/2011/06/celebrating-pride-2011.html.

15   Personal communication (30 August 2013).

16   Personal communication (6 September 2013).

17   Froelich, Jacqueline, 'Gay Walmart group PRIDE comes out', *Arkansas Times*, 12 December 2012. Accessed via the *Arkansas Times* website: http://www.arktimes.com/arkansas/gay-walmart-group-pride-comes-out/Content?oid=2568636.

18 Personal communication (6 December 2013).

19 Human Rights Campaign, *Corporate Equality Index 2014*, p. 30.

20 Human Rights Campaign, *Corporate Equality Index 2006*, p. 8.

21 Personal communication (6 September 2013).

22 Personal communication (24 June 2013).

23 Cowan, Katherine, *Monitoring: How to monitor sexual orientation in the workplace* (Stonewall Workplace Guides, 2006), p. 12.

24 Personal communication (11 September 2013).

25 Personal communication (29 November 2013).

26 Personal communication (2 December 2013).

27 Personal communication (2 June 2013).

28 Hewlett, Sylvia Ann; Sears, Todd; Sumberg, Karen; Fargnoli, Christina, 'The Power of Out 2.0: LGBT in the workplace', Center for Talent Innovation, 2013, p. 35.

29 Personal communication (16 January 2014).

30 Personal communication (10 June 2013).

31 Ashworth, Alice; Lasko, Madeline; Van Vliet, Alex, *Global Working: Supporting lesbian, gay and bisexual staff on overseas assignments* (Stonewall Workplace Guides, 2012), p. 9.

32 Personal communication with Simmons & Simmons (10 January 2014).

33 Personal communication (16 August 2013).

34 Personal communication (14 June 2013).

CHAPTER 9: BEYOND THE CLOSET

1 *The World at One*, BBC Radio 4, 2 December 2013.

2 'Gays in the military: The UK and US compared', BBC News, 2 February 2010. Accessed via the BBC website: http://news.bbc.co.uk/1/hi/8493888.stm.

3 'Gay Tory frontbencher comes out', *The Guardian,* 29 July 2002, Accessed via *The Guardian* website: http://www.theguardian.com/politics/2002/jul/29/conservatives.alanduncan.

4   Macalister, Terry and Carvel, John, 'Diversity drive at BP targets gay staff', *The Guardian*, 20 June 2002. Accessed via *The Guardian* website: http://www.theguardian.com/uk/2002/jun/20/johncarvel.terrymacalister.

5   Chittenden, Maurice, 'Air tycoon breaks City's gay taboo', *The Sunday Times* (of London), 27 October 2002. Accessed via *The Sunday Times* website: http://www.thesundaytimes.co.uk/sto/news/uk_news/article216937.ece.

6   Parris, Matthew, 'Lord Browne paid the price for the City's awkwardness about gays', *The Times* (of London), 2 May 2007. Accessed via *The Times* website: http://www.thetimes.co.uk/tto/opinion/columnists/matthewparris/article2044118.ece.

7   Ibid.

8   Personal correspondence (10 October 2013).

9   Personal communication (3 December 2013).

INDEX